A Short History of the [illegible]*nians*

FÉLIX LUNA

A Short History of the Argentinians

Translated by Cynthia Mansfield
and Ian Barnett

PLANETA
Espejo de la Argentina

This translation is dedicated
to the memory of Cynthia Mansfield.

982 LUN
Luna, Félix
A short history of the argentinians.- 2ª ed. – Buenos Aires : Planeta, 2003.
224 p. ; 22x14 cm.

ISBN 950-49-0403-3

I. Título – 1. Historia Argentina

Diseño de cubierta: María Inés Linares
Diseño de interior: Schavelzon-Ludueña
Estudio de diseño

2ª edición: 3.000 ejemplares

ISBN 950-49-0403-3

Impreso en Cosmos Offset S.R.L.,
Coronel García 444, Avellaneda,
en el mes de marzo de 2003.

Hecho el depósito que prevé la ley 11.723
Impreso en la Argentina

PROLOGUE

Dear Reader,

This book is written in the colloquial style of my lectures so that readers will feel I am having a conversation with them face to face, which is what I would really like to do. It is meant to be spoken, narrated history.

It may seem overambitious to abridge four Argentinian centuries in fifteen chapters but the fact is that history is limitless and, much in the same way as it can be gone into in endless depth, so too can it be summarised.

You will not find many names or dates in this book. Instead my aim is to describe how Argentina has been built up from its foundations through the main periods of its formation. Rather than going into minute detail, I intend to show the major trends and events that have woven Argentinian society and institutions into the country it is today. Rather than being an academic book, this is an overview or, if you like, an introduction to the vast and fascinating terrain of Argentinian history.

F. L.

MAKING HISTORY

The present work sets out to deal with various situations that I feel are significant in the analysis of given historical moments. In the process, I want to shed new light on the present and foster a better understanding of Argentina as it exists today.

As the chapters unfold I shall attempt to answer some of the questions Argentinian society sometimes puts to itself. These questions resemble more personal ones like who we are, what we are here for, what is happening to us, why we are like this and not like that. Naturally, history does not have an answer to all of these questions but it does provide us with a sense of being more firmly rooted in our own reality. Throughout the book I therefore intend to select certain significant events and any act of selection calls for a brief introduction to the methodology employed.

When they use the word "selecting", historians are exercising one of their bewitching powers, namely the ability to assert that "history is the way I tell it". In other words, historians can exercise their gifts for deciding which facts are relevant and which not. A perfect history would be one that spoke of the lives, events and problems of all men at all times. Of course, this would prove to be an impossible venture: even if one were to concentrate on just a single period, it would still be out of the question. The historian's selection is both relative and arbitrary since it is invariably based on an ideology, a set of values and a way of looking at the past.

Nevertheless, such limitations are precisely what makes history exciting: it is never *unique*. There is never just one version that ousts all the others. There is always another possibility, a different point of view, always a way of reading the past from a different viewpoint that teaches us new lessons and bears new fruits.

Another factor to be borne in mind is continuity. History is the aggregate of several combined events and there are times when it seems to gather speed. When this happens and historical events break into a gallop, it is generally the result of confrontations, ideological or otherwise. These clashes make up the raw material closest to historians' hearts, especially where the younger generations are concerned. It is always exciting to depict the struggle between two personalities, ideologies, or powers, yet beneath these momentous confrontations (often, in fact, not as extreme as they might appear) flows an undercurrent of continuities, those processes out of which, silently and on the whole peacefully, the stuff of history is gradually woven.

A good example of this is Juan Domingo Perón, who came to symbolise a break with the established order. He created a political language that was utterly new in Argentina but, in addition to this new approach, he brought with him several elements from the past such as Miguel Miranda's economic plan of 1947, which in turn contained various elements from Pinedo, whose original plan was enforced in 1940 by a conservative government. It is as well then to bear in mind that, between one situation and another, changes have been taking place perhaps imperceptibly, but changes which nevertheless shape a goodly number of historical processes over the years.

CHAPTER I HUMBLE ORIGINS

I shall begin by discussing a key historical moment in the future development of Argentina, and one which also affected Uruguay and Chile (the three countries which together make up America's Southern Cone), namely, the foundation of Buenos Aires. The city of Buenos Aires was in fact founded twice, the first time being forty-four years after the discovery of America. The Rivers Plate and Paraná had first been navigated in 1517 and in 1536 Don Pedro de Mendoza established a small settlement which was to last only a few years.

In the decades to come, settlers moving south from Perú and Alto Perú (an area now occupied by Bolivia) began to populate the northern and central regions of Argentina, whilst other contingents coming from Chile founded the Andean cities of San Juan, Mendoza and San Luis. Other settlers from Asunción had already founded the eastern cities of Santa Fe and Corrientes but it was not until 1580 that Buenos Aires was founded for a second time by Juan de Garay.

BUENOS AIRES: THE GATEWAY

It is important to note that at this early stage the process was one of foundation and colonisation as there were no wars of conquest. The southbound Spaniards had only a very vague notion of the geography in this part of America. What they met with were vast plains interrupted in places by mountain ranges which apart from the Andes were not so forbidding, and wide rivers flowing down from the heart of the continent into the River Plate and on into the Atlantic Ocean. The immensity of the expanses of land and the lack of points of reference presented a challenge to the Spaniards' expertise in cosmography and geography, but one they were eventually able to overcome.

On the eve of the foundation of Buenos Aires there were already three other cities in the territory: Córdoba de la Nueva Andalucía (founded in 1573), Santiago del Estero (1554) and Tucumán (1565). These were poor, provisional settlements, though they were to become cities in their own right with all the bureaucratic formalities in administration peculiar to the Spanish.

On a map of Argentina, these cities are landlocked staging posts facing north or south on the road to and from Alto Perú, or more importantly Potosí. This had won a name for itself as the richest city in America on account of its silver mines and developed into a thriving consumer centre catering not only for get-rich-quick miners but the rest of its population, who depended on the mining industry for a living.

In 1566 Don Juan de Matienzo, a judge in the *Audiencia de Charcas* (Charcas Jurisdiction), which had jurisdiction over the entire southern region, spoke of opening "a gateway to the land". This meant providing the vast expanse stretching south from Potosí to staging posts such as Tucumán, Santiago del Estero and Córdoba with an outlet to the Atlantic. Matienzo had never left Charcas, or Sucre as it is now known, yet he was kept well informed by travellers and maintained that it was essential to establish another settlement where Mendoza had founded the first Buenos Aires. This idea of creating a gateway inland was the original purpose of its second foundation by Juan de Garay, who had been sent by the last governor of the River Plate, or *adelantado* as they were called in Spanish.

And so, in 1580, Buenos Aires was born. However, Garay's foundation did not prove to be as far-reaching as had been expected and after a while it came to be viewed as what a royal accountant would soon describe as "the poorest city in the Indies". In the Spanish Empire it was believed that wealth primarily consisted of gold and silver and Buenos Aires had neither. Before 1610 it was little more than a small village with roughly five hundred inhabitants, castaways in a huge double sea: the Pampas, which they dared not leave as they knew almost nothing beyond the outskirts of the city, and the River Plate which flowed into the Atlantic. This was the wretched plight of the first *Porteños*, or inhabitants of Buenos Aires port, who depended on the arrival of registered ships for their survival.

At this point it would be as well to give a brief description of the Spanish commercial system in those days. In the mid-sixteenth century, fearing pirates and privateers, the Spanish established a system of convoys, which sailed twice a year from Spain and consisted of anything up to fifty galleons escorted by warships.

These convoys followed a precise route usually between Cádiz and the isthmus of Panamá. They would unload their goods in Portobello, send them by mule along the isthmus as far as Panamá City, load them on fresh ships on reaching the Pacific and then, after sailing past Guayaquil, they would put ashore at the port of Callao not far from Lima. There, the merchandise was unloaded and transported by mule and distributed throughout Perú or Alto Perú.

It was a very long haul and the prices of the merchandise accordingly became highly inflated. Still, this was the only system Spain had found to defend itself against attacks from privateers in general, and English privateers in particular. As a result, the Spanish relied exclusively on the strategic ports of Cuba or the isthmus of Panamá. The port of Buenos Aires in the south Atlantic was altogether neglected and only allowed to harbour so-called registered ships, which were authorised to sail once a year or every two years. Anything up to five years could go by without a single registered ship arriving from Spain.

The *Porteños* of Buenos Aires in those days suffered serious privations since they lacked the essential means for survival and production. They had not yet acquired the habits or the techniques for exploiting the resources available in the sprawling Pampas that hemmed them in. And so *Porteños* came to live on bootlegging and smuggling as their only means of survival.

DODGING THE LAW

The contraband came mainly from Brazil. At the time of the foundation of Buenos Aires, after some complicated dynastic manoeuvring, Philip II had annexed the Portuguese crown to that of Spain. He thus became king of Portugal as well, though both kingdoms remained independent. The Portuguese took advantage of their double citizenship and tried to trade with Buenos Aires, which was illegal, their ships not being licensed to put in there. Their vessels were, nevertheless, laden with goods the *Porteños* desperately needed which could be smuggled in anywhere along the endless shores of the River Plate or the Paraná.

Despite the organisation of smuggling over a period of ten or fifteen years, Buenos Aires continued to be a very poor city. The destitution of its citizens has become a legend in its own right. The small band of smugglers was the exception. They had billiard contests, concubines and money to spare. Raúl Molina has given us some amusing stories about the life the smugglers led in glaringly lavish contrast to the indigence of the rest of the population.

Although a few governors such as Hernandarias tried to combat smuggling, such were the inhabitants' needs that the *Porteños* acquired the habit of law-dodging. The fact was that smuggling offered them a better standard of living than did legal channels, which were absurdly contrary to the interests of the city.

At any rate, a community will eventually stumble across a way to make a living, a way of giving its existence a meaning and a purpose. By the early 1600s, Corrientes and Santa Fe had sprung up along the waterway joining Asunción and Buenos Aires. The stages on the overland route, on the other hand, consisted of Buenos Aires, Santa Fe, Córdoba, Santiago del Estero, Tucumán, Salta and Jujuy. This also took in marginal cities like La Rioja and Catamarca, while the province of Cuyo (nowadays the provinces of Mendoza, San Juan and San Luis) was under the jurisdiction of the Captaincy-General of Chile at the time.

Over the years, the network of cities developed and along with it rudimentary differences as regards labour. Each jurisdiction slowly began to specialise in a certain type of production in line with its climate and terrain. There is a letter in the *Archivo de Indias* addressed to the king by a La Rioja resident who wishes to remain anonymous lest he be killed for the denunciations he makes. (Charmingly enough, the organisation in the Indies allowed any subject of the crown to address the king directly by letter using the simple heading

'Señor' and going on to state their requests, denunciations or reports). In his letter dated 1680, our resident of La Rioja proposed that each city within the jurisdictions of Tucumán and Buenos Aires devote itself to its own activities and be forbidden to carry out any other in order to avoid competition. He suggested, for example, that Buenos Aires should produce mules, clothes and furniture, that La Rioja should only trade in wines and aguardiente, Catamarca in textiles, Santiago del Estero in textiles and mules, Córdoba in clothing and so on.

Where did Buenos Aires come into the picture? Its business was smuggling, which meant that it became the back door for all illegal trade. This trade then spread north to Tucumán, a jurisdiction comprising the present-day provinces of Córdoba, Santiago del Estero, Tucumán, Jujuy, Salta, La Rioja and Catamarca. The entire jurisdiction of Tucumán was much larger than that of Buenos Aires, (which took in Buenos Aires province, part of Santa Fe and present-day Uruguay and parts of southern Brazil, or the Banda Oriental as it was known) and was ruled by a governor residing in Santiago del Estero.

In the early 1600s, the readiest source of wealth with which *Porteños* could purchase smuggled goods, was the huge unclaimed herds that roamed the Pampas. In the countryside near Buenos Aires, and in the south of the provinces of Santa Fe and Córdoba, live-stock had been reproducing on an extraordinary scale and the inhabitants of Buenos Aires set up partnerships for the so-called *vaquerías*, or cattle-hunting expeditions carried out by men armed with spears. Ten or fifteen rugged countrymen willing to put up with the harsh life-style and earn a good few reals would set out in search of stray animals. When they found the unclaimed cattle, they would nick their shanks with the tip of a sickle-shaped rod and the beast would fall to the ground immobilised. The second step was to slit the throats of the hundreds of struggling beasts and skin them.

The only part they took was the animals' hides, which were loaded onto huge wagons, taken to be tanned and then shipped abroad. That was the sum total of *Porteño* exports. The rest was all thrown away: the meat, the horns, the tallow... One can picture the Pampas strewn with carcasses scavenged by wild dogs and rats, the plague of the countryside.

There were several reasons why the *vaquerías* were important. They were the first *Porteño* industry regardless of how primitive or wasteful it may seem to us. Nowadays, they would be considered outrageous from an environmental point of view, but in those days this was the only form of barter available. In fact, this early means of production would develop into today's highly sophisticated meat-freezing industry. But the *vaquerías* were also important because they gradually established the political borders of what would become some of today's provinces. Inhabitants of Santa Fe would often hunt for cattle in the jurisdiction of Buenos Aires whereupon the *Cabildo* (Town Council) of Buenos Aires would angrily accuse them of trespassing. There were similar disputes with Córdoba as well.

Eventually, around 1720, the *cabildos* of Santa Fe and Buenos Aires finally agreed to establish the Arroyo del Medio (literally the Middle Stream) as the border that still divides both provinces, and likewise with the town council in Córdoba.

JEALOUSY AND RIVALRIES

Another feature typical of the early days of Buenos Aires is that right from its very foundation it stirred up a series of feuds. In spite of its out-and-out poverty and the quaint form of its livelihood, it was strategically situated from a geographical point of view; "the gateway to the land" that Matienzo had dreamed of, and in this sense its main rival was Lima.

It was obvious (and many a functionary said so at the time) that the shortest and easiest way to transport goods was to cross the Atlantic, put in at Buenos Aires and then send the merchandise overland to Alto Perú, there being hardly any mountains or rivers blocking the way across the plains. There was a perfect overland route from Buenos Aires to Potosí but the other, from Cádiz to Portobello along the isthmus of Panamá, which involved unloading and shipping the wares down through the Pacific to Callao and on to Lima, was an extremely costly complication.

For example, in 1778 when an *Auto de Libre Comercio* (License for Free Trade) was obtained, it was estimated that a yard of linen shipped to Potosí by the longest route would be sold at about thirty pesos a metre whereas, if it reached Potosí via Buenos Aires, it would cost no more than five pesos.

Lima, controlling the black slave trade, squared up to Buenos Aires from the outset. When the South Sea Company settled in Argentina in 1720 as a result of the Treaty of Utrecht, England opened an overseas slave-trading post in Buenos Aires and Lima came down heavily on the Argentine city authorities. Lima, with the Viceroy of Perú's backing, had already quite rightly complained about the fact that Buenos Aires was not only a back door for incoming contraband but also for illegal exports of silver from the mining city of Potosí, and that this was proving to be an uncontrollable drain on the exchequer.

Rivalry with Lima led to the setting up of an inland custom-house at Córdoba in around 1620 for the arduous task of controlling goods arriving in the city. However, there was a road from Buenos Aires crossing the territory of Santa Fe and skirting the city of Córdoba which made it perfectly possible to avoid the new customs. After much controversy, Lima moved the customs office to Santiago del Estero and finally, after more sound and fury in bureaucratic spheres, to Jujuy in 1680 or 90.

Such then was the emergence of a domestic market which would later define the borders of Argentina. Except for the Buenos Aires customs office, which was entirely devoted to smuggling, the business of bringing goods all the way into Jujuy was virtually a single market, and markets often prove to be a prerequisite for the building of a nation. History was laying the foundations for what was later to become the territory of Argentina.

Buenos Aires vied with other cities, too: with Santa Fe over the *vaquerías* and, from around 1730, with Montevideo. When it was founded, many people observed that Montevideo had a far better port than existed in Buenos Aires. It lacked the latter's tuff and shallows. Indeed, it began to be regarded as the true gateway to the land, even though dispatching goods from Montevideo involved crossing two great rivers, the Paraná and the River Plate.

Competition between the two cities was spurred on to such an extent that in 1804 the consulate in Buenos Aires (which consisted of little more than an assembly of *Porteño* tradesmen) fell out over the building of a lighthouse in the port of Montevideo. The tense relationships between the two cities also explain why Montevideo was later to become one of the Spanish crown's strongholds against Argentina's independence struggle, the *Revolución de Mayo* of 1810. A counter-revolution was set up in Montevideo lasting until 1814, when Carlos María de Alvear managed to take the Uruguayan city by storm. It is also worth mentioning that the long-standing rivalry with Perú came to the fore at the time of Argentina's independence, when Lima became the last royalist bastion in South America (either out of true loyalty to Spain, or as an expression of the old ill-feeling).

To recap, the city of Buenos Aires was founded in 1580, lived on illegal trade and developed a habit of cheating the law. Its production was based on an ecological catastrophe, in other words the indiscriminate decimation of whole herds of cattle. The situation had become so serious by 1715 that the city council banned the *vaquerías* because "if things go on like this, our hides will be tanned...". And they were right!

THE ORGANISING POWER OF BUENOS AIRES

In spite of the feuds and rivalries Buenos Aires aroused in the rest of the provinces, it also developed a certain degree of power and influence over them. This became clear when in 1680 a Portuguese expedition landed and established a settlement at Colonia del Sacramento and Buenos Aires came up against the might of Portugal.

The Portuguese and Spanish crowns had separated only a few years before and Portugal aspired to holding the south of Brazil and the territory up to the River Plate under its sway. Colonia on the south coast of Uruguay, was the key to the Rivers Paraná and Uruguay as well as to the River Plate and was the only rocky part of the shoreline. It was, in other words, the perfect place for fortifications.

When the governor of Buenos Aires, José de Garro, learnt about the settlement, he sent a rasping ultimatum to the head of the Portuguese expedition, Manuel de Lobo. In it he warned him that the Banda Oriental belonged to the King of Spain and urged him to leave. Lobo in his turn asked the governor to allow him to set up camp and let any diplomatic affairs be dealt with before the courts. He said that his intentions were entirely peaceful and that his aim was to trade with Buenos Aires. José de Garro, an extremely stubborn Basque and a patriot, insisted that they abandon Colonia del Sacramento, and this gave rise to a very curious phenomenon.

De Garro summoned "the live forces" in Buenos Aires (consisting of the secular city council, the ecclesiastical city council, the foremost tradesmen, the king's officials, all the most important men) to consult them about what course of action to adopt. All agreed that the Portuguese foundation had to be attacked and the usurpers expelled, so de Garro sent a circular to his counterpart in Tucumán urging him to move their militia to Buenos Aires and set about driving out the Portuguese.

And indeed contingents did arrive from Córdoba, Tucumán and La Rioja. They had been gathered by Buenos Aires' feudatory neighbours, as those holding *encomiendas* were called, a system whereby governors were allotted local labour. One of their feudatory obligations was to serve the king at their own expense whenever military action was required. De Garro also asked the Jesuits to send along Guaraní Indians as reinforcements, which all told made up a three thousand-strong army, led by Antonio de Vera y Mujica, a *criollo* born in Santa Fe. (The Spanish *criollo*, or 'creole', was used to signify someone of Spanish extraction born in the Americas.)

When the military force had been organised, José de Garro summoned the high-ranking citizens of Buenos Aires once again to decide whether the expedition should go ahead regardless of the fact that Portugal and Spain were at peace and that driving out the Portuguese could result in a serious diplomatic incident. The assembly agreed to attack and the course of events led to a gruesome massacre. The native Guaranís particularly resented the Portuguese because of the *bandeirantes*' raids on them (another story altogether) and killed most of the settlers who were in fact mainly peace-loving ploughmen.

Manuel de Lobo himself was taken prisoner and died a couple of years later.

The significance of all this lies in the fact that, although Buenos Aires was one hundred years old by then, it lacked the status of Córdoba, which already had a university, or of Santiago del Estero, which was the oldest city in the country, or Asunción, which had been the leading South American city in the early days. However, Buenos Aires, with its burden of poverty and lawlessness, managed to call together the rest of the population for what was tantamount to Argentina's first war. It was a fight against a foreign enemy usurping Spanish property and most of the men who went to war were *criollos*. The soldiers of the Tucumán militia, who were the grandchildren or great-grandchildren of the conquistadors, and with them the Guaranís, they were all commanded by a *criollo* of Spanish descent.

Out of the blue Buenos Aires had acquired a prestige that would later be enhanced by the creation of the Viceroyalty of the River Plate, its resistance against the English Invasions and the *Revolución de Mayo*. A city that had been born and raised in lawlessness, relied on outlandish *vaquerías* to maintain its economy, one that aroused feuding and rivalry, nevertheless had enough organising influence to oust the Portuguese usurpers and to obtain the co-operation of other cities in that part of South America.

At the same time, the provinces were also growing and specialising in certain areas: Tucumán took advantage of its high-quality wood to manufacture wagons; in Santiago del Estero, the abundant supply of indigenous labour allowed a rudimentary yet significant textile industry, while Córdoba specialised in breeding mules, which were then sent on to Salta and sold for use in the mines in Alto Perú and Perú.

The provinces were permanently harassed by the Indians from the Chaco, who in fact occupied part of Salta, Jujuy and present-day Formosa, but more importantly Santiago del Estero and Santa Fe, and posed a constant threat to the cities and towns in Tucumán. Because of this threat every governor called on their citizens' assistance in waging expeditions against the Indians, subduing them and generally inspiring fear. Córdoba almost always answered the call; Santiago del Estero reacted enthusiastically because its own interests were at stake, and Salta and Jujuy were also eager to cooperate. La Riojans and Catamarcans were rather more reluctant, because the Chaco was so far away. But the *Porteños* of Buenos Aires never co-operated and this annoyed the cities of the provinces. In the context of this provincial solidarity, Buenos Aires was always the odd man out. It repeatedly came up with one excuse after another, such as spotting pirates on the coast or seeing to its own problems. The attitude of the *Porteños* created a difference of political interests between Buenos Aires and those of the other cities.

POLITICAL ORGANISATION

At this point, it would be as well to give a brief description of the political and legal form of organisation in these latitudes. In point of fact, this was not so different from that of the Spanish empire: some of the New World authorities had been set up as straightforward copies of the Spanish system.

As an example of this, let us look at the *adelantados*, or advance agents. During the eight years of the Reconquest, Castille and León's struggle against the Moors, the kings would appoint a nobleman as an advance agent in extending the Christian frontier at the Moors' expense, often for sheer lack of money. In exchange, the crown conferred certain privileges on them, as they were to do on the *adelantados* settling the new territories.

The first *adelantado* in the River Plate was Pedro de Mendoza. Others were sent to other regions of South America. The *adelantado* signed a contract whereby he committed himself to covering all the expedition's expenses, in exchange for which he was made a captain-general and judge. He was also granted certain privileges of command and power, and a portion of the land to be explored. Within less than a century the system had proved to be a dangerous flop. Due to the huge distances that separated them from Madrid and because of their temperaments; *adelantados* tended to be absolutely independent operators, as had been the case with Pizarro and Lope de Aguirre in Perú.

The practice was cancelled and bureaucrats sent in their stead; first governors and then viceroys. The governors were in charge of the larger jurisdictions, such as Tucumán, Paraguay and Buenos Aires and were answerable to the viceroy, which in our case meant the viceroy of Perú in Lima.

The Viceroyalty of Lima was set up shortly after the Conquest, as was the case in Mexico. The authority was a direct representative of the king, usually a knight or a nobleman who were generally capable and efficient men. This institution marked the beginning of what might be called an Executive Power, which moreover at times encroached upon the judiciary.

Another important institution besides that of viceroy was the *Audiencia*, a kind of high court of justice, which took care of judicial affairs. Its members, figures such as Juan de Matienzo, were expected to convey their queries to the king and were also in charge of planning. Thus, the function of these courts stretched beyond strictly judicial affairs to functions of government.

Then there were the *cabildos*, or city councils responsible for municipal government. It should be born in mind that every city was founded by the Crown in the name of the Crown, whereas in North America settlers arrived as free citizens or as colonising companies selling land and then founding cities. In South America, where everything was done in the name of the Crown, the founder would appoint the first members of the city council (usually between six and ten, according to the city's size) each of whom had a different function. It was a great honour to be a member of the *cabildo*; their term lasted one year and then they themselves appointed their successors. They were not voted into office by popular consent, as happened in some North American states.

In theory the *cabildos* looked after municipal affairs but because cities were so far apart, in practice they carried out the political functions of government as well. When there were droughts, they had to take measures to supply the population with provisions; when local Indians attacked, they had to take military action; and if the governor abused his power, they would lodge official complaints to the viceroy.

In the colonies' power structure, another important institution was the Church. This played a political role besides its strictly religious one, controlling, overseeing, lodging complaints and basically imparting some degree of balance between the powers-that-be.

As far as the political organisation of the colonies was concerned, no branches of power were clearly defined. Nowadays, we would kick up a fuss if the judiciary started meddling in political affairs; however, in those days an *audiencia* had the power to replace the viceroy, as indeed happened in Buenos Aires in 1806. It could also take political action just as the viceroy could take judicial action as the president of the *Audiencia*.

This situation did not arise by chance. The Spanish crown tried to maintain a certain state of confusion in order to keep overall control of the colonies. In the event of abuse or excessive independence, some other body could set things straight. It was a highly delicate system of political counterweights governed by the laws of the Indies, which moreover were casuistic in that their only general principle was to seek the common good.

The organisation in South America was born of old Spanish Law, whose main asset was the idea that everything should be done to benefit the community. This philosophical principle had interesting practical applications: if, when a viceroy received royal letters patent from the king in Madrid and upon reading it he considered it nonsense, he would solemnly summon the functionaries, the city council, the *Audiencia* and the bishop and state "It shall be observed but not executed" or, in other words, "We acknowledge the authority of the person stating this, but as it does not contribute to the common good and would do more harm than good, we will not carry it out but file it away in a drawer instead".

This was normal procedure, which meant that the authorities of a colony exercised a kind of veto over the king's decisions. The monarch may have been recognised as the supreme authority, but could also at times be rather badly informed about the real state of affairs in South America. After the May Revolution, this privileging of the common good would be replaced by the sovereignty of the people.

INDIANS

The backdrop to all this was the Indian presence, which colours, enhances and animates the whole picture. The existence of aboriginal peoples in the New World brought upheavals in both Spain and Europe. The fact that a 'new' continent had been discovered in which there were living beings, who were eventually recognised as human beings, posed a number of serious problems for theology, philosophy, the Law, politics and science.

The kind of questions that arose were things like "If they are human beings, has Christ saved them? Do we have to evangelise them? Do we have an obligation to baptise them? Is it part of our mission to do so?". Which boiled down to the question "Do we have any right to fight wars against them, deprive them of their belongings, enslave them and generally make the most of them?" These issues were discussed in Spain on various occasions: theologians held meetings and many books were written on the subject. Under what circumstances could Spain go to war against Indians who had done her no wrong? The Spanish were the invaders and what right did they have to fight them?

During the first years of the conquest this problem remained by and large a theoretical one. But when Hernán Cortés disembarked on the shores of Mexico in 1519 and for the first time in the history of European civilisation came face to face with an unknown culture possibly more advanced and more affluent than their own, the issue of the Indians presented itself quite differently. What to do with the Indians and how to make the most of them were the new concerns. The Conquest was already a fact of life and there was no stopping it.

How could they be exploited without committing a sin that might burden the Spanish conscience? This is why the Spanish institution called the *encomienda* (from the Spanish verb *encomendar* meaning 'to entrust') was invented: to defend the population of South America in general (with the exception of Buenos Aires, which had no Indians in thrall) and Tucumán in particular. An *encomienda* consisted in 'entrusting' a Spaniard with a group of Indians, a few Indian families or a whole tribe in order to save their souls and provide them with minimum welfare. In exchange, the Indians had to work for the Spaniards or, after 1615, pay them a tithe.

Citizens who had this privilege were expected to serve the king whenever it was deemed necessary and they gradually came to wield the power of feudal lords, since the Indians they were entrusted with were not their slaves and could not be swapped, sold or moved.

This was what the overall picture in Tucumán and Buenos Aires was like around the mid-eighteenth century, by which time these social and political structures were well-established. Also around this time the Bourbon dynasty was growing stronger in Spain and European nations were changing their idea of wealth and the value of colonial possessions. This brings us to the eve of the creation of the Viceroyalty of the River Plate.

CHAPTER II THE COLONIAL PERIOD

Before getting down to the specifics involved in the creation of the Viceroyalty of the River Plate, I will set down a few of the developments from the mid-eighteenth century that I think may be of interest.

We left off this chronicle at the turn of the eighteenth century around the time of the death of Charles II, the War of the Spanish Succession and the coronation of Philip V, the first Bourbon monarch. Between then and the beginning of this chapter some events originating in the previous century took on greater significance.

THE *ESTANCIAS*

Buenos Aires began to change, not so much the city itself as its environs. Its inhabitants in the early days lived like sailors shipwrecked between two huge seas, the Pampas and the River Plate. By the mid-eighteenth century, indigenous peoples probably from Chile had discovered the horse and occupied the empty spaces in the Pampas, thus posing a threat to the Christian population.

As a result, the inhabitants of Buenos Aires strove to protect the few settlements surrounding them by creating villages defended by small mud buildings or stockades. Mercedes, San Miguel del Monte, Chascomús, Dolores are just some names in a line of forts stretching all the way to Melincué. They were manned by civilians drafted into a sort of militia nicknamed the *blandengues* or 'softies'. Despite being badly paid and poorly armed, it was they who formed the first line of defence in the event of an Indian raid.

The purpose of this small circle of forts was to protect the first *estancias* (the vast cattle ranches on the outskirts of Buenos Aires) from Indian raids. Until that time agricultural wealth, which consisted predominantly of cattle, had come from herds simply being hunted down in the *vaquerías*. But as the ownerless cattle herds were seriously depleted by the early eighteenth century, some *Porteños* began setting up stations for domesticating them so that they were to hand at slaughtering-time.

The most common way of keeping the cattle together on these new estates was with a *rascadero*. This was an imposing post pitched in the middle of the Pampas, so called because it was where the animals would go to scratch themselves (*rascadero* comes from *rascar*, the Spanish word for 'to scratch'). It is mentioned in the national Gaucho epic, *Martín Fierro*, as "the post to go and scratch yourself on". The cattle could drink there and may have been left some salt loaves to balance out their diet of grass. Near the *rascadero* stood the owner's ranch-house and sometimes that of his deputy or foreman. *Estancieros* lived wild and solitary lives. They were many days' journey from Buenos Aires where they could find the necessary provisions. In fact, as far as relationships and work were concerned, *estancieros* led lives not dissimilar to the local Indians'.

Despite this precarious existence, the *estancias* of Buenos Aires began to take shape. Their basic product was leather, which had been the chief quarry of the *vaquerías* and was being processed in ever more refined ways. It was tanned on the premises and shipped out at fairly regular intervals. Occasionally a few by-products such as horns or hoofs were thrown in for good measure.

Leather, being a crucial household commodity in those days, was used amongst other things for lining axles on cartwheels, for horses' harnesses or accessories on uniforms (not only shoes and boots but belts and cartridge belts). Furniture or carriages of a certain distinction were upholstered in leather and it was compulsory in the best cloakrooms. Especially when there was a war on, leather was needed to pack and line cannon and the *estancias* springing up near Buenos Aires, shielded from the Indians by a cinch of forts, were answering an ever increasing demand, not least from Europe.

The countenance of Buenos Aires, a God-forsaken city which had been living off contraband or waiting for a registered ship to arrive every couple of years, was slowly changing. By the mid-eighteenth century, it had undergone a sea change thanks to its land-based leather industry. By the later eighteenth century a society was gradually emerging in which people were valued for who they were and what they had. Social worth was not measured in surnames or birthright but in people's achievements.

Meanwhile in the provinces other changes were taking place: the sense of selfhood in cities such as Córdoba, Mendoza (which still belonged to the Chilean Captaincy-General), La Rioja and San Miguel de Tucumán was growing stronger. Tucumán and Mendoza, for instance, produced wagons of quite distinct appearance. Thus each city came to specialise in one particular type of production, which provided each of them in their turn with a specific identity and bound the members of their communities together.

JESUITS

Both politically and ideologically, the Bourbon dynasty was all about absolutism. In the mid-eighteenth century, Bourbon policies had repercussions throughout this part of America. Two events stand out, the first of which is the expulsion of the Jesuits in 1767.

Within the Spanish empire the Jesuit order had established a quite remarkable enclave. This covered part of present-day Paraguay, Corrientes in north-eastern Argentina and the Brazilian and Uruguayan shores of the River Uruguay, and took in approximately seventy Guaraní towns. The Guaranís had abandoned their nomadic habits and were governed by Jesuit fathers strictly trained by the Society of Jesus to become administrators of these towns.

I believe we should pay homage to these priests' intentions. They were quite simply heroic. They identified with the Guaranís to such an extent that they even adopted their language in place of Spanish; they rescued them from their itinerant lifestyle, civilised them, taught them trades, unified their language and made them the authors of many cultural expressions of both beauty and practical value.

I have sometimes thought that towards the middle of the seventeenth century the Jesuits must have said to themselves something like "We no longer have anything to do in Europe. That civilisation is corrupted by profit, greed and cruelty. Let us find a place to try out a completely different kind of civilisation, one in which the spirit of profit does not exist, where people work for each others' benefit and nobody has any money because they have no need for it; somewhere people can live as brothers and sisters." From a certain point of view the regime in Jesuit towns can, economically speaking, be described as socialist. No one possessed anything of their own other than basic household items and everybody's needs were met by the community "from each according to his abilities, to each according to his needs."

The Jesuit presence on Argentine territory also had a political dimension: they defended Spanish territory against Portuguese-led raiding parties, the so-called *bandeirantes* from Brazil, and stubbornly opposed a move to barter away seven Guaraní towns to Brazil in exchange for the Portuguese-held Colonia del Sacramento.

But it was precisely the Jesuits' political clout that presented the Spanish crown with a problem. Many thousands of Guaranís lived in Jesuit towns and some of them had military training. In other words they might constitute a significant military threat. Consequently, in 1767 Charles III sent secret orders to the authorities of all the Spanish colonies to take all the Jesuits under their jurisdiction into safekeeping and make an inventory of their possessions.

In mid-1767, a month after Charles' order had been issued, squads of armed men banged on the doors of Jesuit residences, which were not confined to Misiones where their most famous ruins stand today, but were scattered throughout Argentina. The soldiers detained the priests and seized their goods. For almost a century, the Society of Jesus vanished from what is now Argentine soil.

The event had untold ramifications. All the cultural activity that had been marshalled by the Jesuits ceased, not only in the missions but elsewhere in Argentine territory. Other religious orders tried to fill the gap left by the Society of Jesus, whose worldly possessions were sold off or auctioned. From these sales there emerged a new kind of proprietor in the provinces, one with a higher social and political standing: having been acquired by a gentleman by the name of Díaz, the splendid ranch of Santa Catalina, a former Jesuit possession near Jesús María in Córdoba became one of the most significant cattle enterprises of its day.

The Jesuits could not last very long in this territory for one reason: because their prosperity invited the greed of some of the Spanish officials who presumed that the settlements of the converted Guaranís should be Crown heritage. The Jesuits' error may well have been not to teach the Guaranís to govern themselves. The proof that they were not able to do so lies in the fact that, after the Jesuits were expelled, the missions fell into utter ruin. Despite the Franciscan fathers taking them over in all eagerness, their cultural heritage was dissipated relatively quickly. By 1782, from what had been a hive of industry just fifteen years before virtually nothing remained.

However that may be, the achievements of the Jesuit missions during their hundred-and-fifty-year experiment was truly admirable. The church of La Compañía in Córdoba, the ranches of Jesús María and Santa Catalina and the Candonga chapel, are just some of their chapels and churches that can still be seen to this day. The Jesuits even managed to set up a wooden printing press in the middle of the jungle and print books which are graphic marvels even by today's standards. The press was later moved to Córdoba and from there, at the time of the Jesuits' expulsion, to the Imprenta de los Niños Expósitos (the Foundlings Press) in Buenos Aires, which has since produced so many titles.

There were other factors too which motivated the Society's expulsion: Masonic elements operating in the heart of the Portuguese and Spanish governments; the theories of the Encyclopedists; the liberal ideas already rampant in Europe. Moreover, there were financial scandals which had smeared the Jesuit name and weakened the order in France. You have to look no further than Voltaire's *Candide* to see how far the Society had become the object of calumny, and the criticisms were sometimes well-founded.

Several European states such as Russia or Poland subsequently opened their doors to the Jesuits. Some moved to Italy, particularly to Faenza; some wrote works of beauty about their experiences in America; others stayed behind to celebrate the advent of Independence, either because they loathed Spanish rule for expelling them or out of their long-standing affection for America. Still others like Villafañe, an Argentine from La Rioja, returned to the River Plate after Independence. Their lives were pretty miserable by and large after the dissolution. They had been used to being part of an extremely close-knit body which had suddenly been scattered across the world. The order was not reformed until the eighteenth century.

CHANGES

The other significant change relating to Bourbon absolutism was the onset of a more strictly fiscalist regime and one which met with greater resistance in this part of South America. On the Crown's part, there was a need to introduce reforms in the interest of stronger government. This in turn led to a more colonial regime: orders were even given to destroy any olive plantations or tobacco crops competing with Spanish oil and tobacco.

Previously, under the Hapsburg dynasty, America had been contributing only twenty per cent of its metals (the so-called royal fifth) to the Spanish crown, the rest being left for private individuals. After the Bourbons a more rational fiscal regime was implemented. Moreover, a change in the conception of the wealth of nations was coming about: instead of believing, as was previously the case, that this consisted solely in gold and silver, goods such as leather and economic activity in general began to be considered as wealth. The River Plate region, which had no gold nor silver but did possess other assets, began to be prized more highly.

The colonial regime never found its full expression because it was interrupted by the Independence movement. At the time of the English Invasions, Spain's military weakness in America became clear for all to see. But even before the invasions Spain had proved unable to oil the wheels of the American economy because it lacked a proper fleet. Charles III and his successors strove to rebuild both the naval and merchant fleets with some success; the mercantile economy demanded it.

Also important was the Portuguese advance into the River Plate area. We have already described how Buenos Aires mustered a national expeditionary force to drive the Portuguese out of Colonia del Sacramento. This event gave rise to a series of diplomatic and military manoeuvres and the Spanish were to seize Colonia on several occasions only to hand it back later after diplomatic treaties had been signed. Eventually the *Tratado de Permuta* (Treaty of Exchange) was signed, according to which Spain would cede seven mission towns in exchange for Colonia. But in 1776, Don Pedro de Cevallos, later to become the first Viceroy of the River Plate, arrived at the head of a huge expeditionary force, the largest yet to be seen in America. His mission was to secure Colonia once and for all and reinforce the borders between Portugal and Spain.

VICEROYALTY

In 1776 the Viceroyalty of the River Plate was formed. Until then Buenos Aires as a governing body had been separate from Tucumán. Both had been dependent, at least in theory, on the Viceroyalty of Lima. After 1776 both jurisdictions became part of the Viceroyalty of Buenos Aires, together with Paraguay and the Cuyo region which used to answer to the Captaincy-General of Chile. The grand design for a great nation was roughed out and Buenos Aires came of age.

The most significant event from an institutional angle is the appointment of Don Pedro de Cevallos as Viceroy of the River Plate by royal order. This put him in charge of an area which included Alto Perú and the governments of old Tucumán and Paraguay. There were several cities in these regions that were well qualified to become the capital of the new Viceroyalty: Córdoba had been the seat of the most prestigious university in that part of America since 1615; Potosí, whose legendary wealth had filled the coffers of Spain for more than a century, still had mythical prestige; Asunción del Paraguay had been the first city to be founded in those parts.

The Spanish court decided on Buenos Aires despite its peripheral location because it was ideal to ward off any future Portuguese advance and had besides the easiest access to Spain across the Atlantic. A strong *Porteño* lobby in Madrid might also have contributed to Buenos Aires' selection as the flagship of the new Viceroyalty, which was to be the last of its kind in America. Its jurisdiction stretched across the present-day republics of Argentina, Uruguay, Bolivia and Paraguay.

Buenos Aires may have been the capital but the other cities had their own jurisdiction. These municipal governments or *cabildos* were communal and were responsible for the common good, for affairs that went beyond the strictly municipal and by 1810 they were exercising considerable political power. Many of these governments were composed of *criollos*, whose Spanish ancestry dated back a good few generations.

Subsequently, municipal jurisdictions began establishing de facto the approximate boundaries of today's countries and provinces on a basis of *uti possidetis*, a legacy of Spanish civilisation. This is a principle of American international law meaning "as ye possessed". Whenever there is a border dispute between American countries, the Spanish archives are consulted first to find out what the Spanish jurisdiction was. If this is clearly drawn, it is taken as a border. Thus, for example the border between Bolivia and Peru is the River Desaguadero, because that was where the Viceroyalty of the River Plate stopped and the Viceroyalty of Peru began.

The Viceroyalty of the River Plate had an outlet to both the Atlantic and the Pacific, the latter through the Puno region where the Chilean-Bolivian border is today. It covered a vast area containing two great rivers, the Paraná and the Uruguay, and immeasurable prairies suitable for any kind of agriculture. In terms of economic potential, forty thousand mules a year were bred in the region north of Buenos Aires, south of Córdoba and south of Santa Fe and including Entre Ríos. These were then taken to Salta to be sold to the miners of Perú and Alto Perú. In Misiones, Paraguay and the north of Corrientes and Tucumán there were magnificent forests which allowed all kinds of wood-based manufactures at a time when this was a prized building material. There were mineral deposits in Alto Perú and silver and other minerals in Mendoza.

The new viceroyalty was large enough to be self-sufficient and lasted some thirty years. But it took in regions which were all too diverse and had to establish by force any political links between territories whose inhabitants were ethnically of widely differing customs, origins and needs. Alto Perú, whose social, commercial and political ties had for centuries been with Lima, was suddenly joined to Buenos Aires. A similar situation existed in the Cuyo region which had traditionally been dependent on Santiago de Chile and suddenly belonged to a capital more than a thousand kilometres away. Or Montevideo, which had its sights on being the leading port in the region.

The Viceroyalty of the River Plate really needed longer than it had to consolidate its position. In fact, its component regions were so incompatible that, when after 1810 links with Spain were severed, it quite simply burst apart at the seams forming the republics of Argentina, Bolivia, Paraguay and Uruguay. Still, it had been conceived on a grand scale. Its expanse was roughly that of the United States and its two outlets to the Atlantic and Pacific potentially meant that it was connected to the whole world. Patagonia and the Malvinas Islands fell within its jurisdiction and with them the lucrative prospect of fishing, seal-hunting and whaling.

PROSPERITY

1776 marked the beginning of a period of prosperity for Buenos Aires and to an extent for outlying areas such as the old government of Tucumán which benefited from the *Auto de Libre Internación* (Free Internment Edict) and the *Reglamento de Libre Comercio* (Free Trade Regulations) of 1777 and 1778 respectively. After the creation of the Viceroyalty of the River Plate, trade became all in all much more open, flexible and liberal.

The Free Trade Regulations granted the port of Buenos Aires direct links with the ports of Spain and most of America without having to obtain prior authorisation. Merchandise could be brought into both old Tucumán and Alto Perú. Thus colonial ties between this jurisdiction and the Viceroyalty of Lima were severed, provoking bitter protests not only from the inhabitants of Lima but also from its viceroys, who reached the point of asking the Spanish crown to overrule the creation of the fledgling Viceroyalty.

After the new rulings, the influx of goods through the port of Buenos Aires shot up. Between 1780 and 1800 the city underwent a veritable spate of developments (as it would a hundred years on between 1880 and 1910, a period still present in the collective memory). In these years many immigrants (mostly Spanish but also Italians, French and other nationalities) settled in Buenos Aires. The port received vessels from North America, whalers or ships bringing wheat. An extremely lively exchange sprang up; the *casas de comercio* (trading-houses) were on the up and up, and breathed life into a middle class who would, decades later, have an important say in Buenos Aires politics.

There were many cases of young men, often not much more than teenagers, being sent by their families in Spain to *Porteño* trading-houses. The future mayor of Buenos Aires, Martín de Alzaga, who would later play such a crucial role in fighting off the English, was a Basque who spoke no Spanish on his arrival in the city. The founders of time-honoured old families such as the Lezicas or the Anchorenas all started out life like this. They arrived in Buenos Aires appointed to a trading-house where they worked as clerks or salesmen for a few years. They would often marry the boss's daughter, acquire social standing and later be chosen as *cabildantes* (city councillors). They would receive honours and wealth and their children become army officers. Their grandchildren were the emphyteutas, or rent-paying landholders, of the first president of the Argentine Republic, Bernardino Rivadavia, and were friends of J.M. de Rosas, the Federalist governor of Buenos Aires Province. Their great-grandchildren would do very nicely out of Julio A. Roca, the Indian-slaying conqueror of Patagonia, and after Roca (since family fortunes in Argentina tend not to last much more than two generations) they would all be bankrupt...

Back at the end of the eighteenth century, Buenos Aires packed a large number of traders and apprentices into the *casas de comercio*. To get some idea of what these were like, one might recall the first chapter of Alejo Carpentier's novel *El siglo de las luces* (Explosion in a Cathedral) where he describes the main characters' arrival in Havana: they went into the warehouses and took in the aromas: dried fish, cod, though probably not *yerba mate*, unknown in Cuba though *de rigueur* in Buenos Aires. It gives us a glimpse of what the neighbourhood around the Buenos Aires docks near the Plaza de Mayo would be like. This was where the depositories stood and here goods were traded, later to be carted off to the likes of Córdoba, Misiones and Salta.

At around the same time, a class sprang up in Buenos Aires that had the odd aristocratic urge though being made up primarily of commoners. This was a society of traders and ranchers who were either on their way up or had already made it, though many of them still led a life on their ranches that was just as tough and wild as it had been forty years earlier when the forts were being built.

Nevertheless, *Porteño* society lacked the aristocratic prejudice of for example Córdoba with its rigidly exclusive, colonial approach to society. Concolorcorvo, the pseudonym of a *mestizo* (half-caste) whose name translates rather graphically as 'crow-coloured', had to make the journey from Buenos Aires to Lima and choose the best places to set up staging-posts for the mail. He records these different attitudes to class in his book *El lazarillo de ciegos caminantes* (The Guide for Blind Travellers).

Here he tells the reader that in Buenos Aires there weren't the prejudices of breeding he noticed in the provincial cities. He points out that in Córdoba, if *mestizo* girls dressed like women of a certain standing, the "ladies" would get together and gave them a good hiding, strip them naked and made a laughing stock out of them. In Buenos Aires however, it was possible for a hard-working immigrant like Manuel Belgrano's father arriving from Genoa to make some money and even send his son to study in Spain. Financial success reaped honours and social prestige, and this set Buenos Aires apart from the provinces. There ancestry was still all-important and the conquistadors' *criollo* descendents held their ground on their unprofitable, musty ranches.

There were other differences, too. Buenos Aires benefited from the way the viceroyalty was organised in that, over such an enormous territory, some cities had to be supervised by the viceroy's representatives for the distant centre's authority to be felt. So-called *intendencias* (mayoralties) were set up in Córdoba and Salta, Alto Perú and Asunción amongst other places.

The *intendencias*, administered by government officials (some of whom, such as the Marquis of Sobremonte in Córdoba, were remembered with affection), in turn had other places under their jurisdiction. Cities like San Juan, Mendoza, La Rioja and Catamarca came under the administration of Córdoba, while San Miguel de Tucumán came under the auspices of Salta. Their diminished status began to smart, so they attempted to by-pass cities that were *intendencias* and appeal directly to Buenos Aires. As a result, the capital became something akin to a protector of the smaller cities and the outright rival of Córdoba and Salta.

All this goes some way to explaining why the Independence struggles of 1810 were met with a counter-revolution in Córdoba and why Salta's adherence to the *Junta de Mayo* was quite some time in coming. However that may be, Buenos Aires had finally achieved its founding ambition of being the gateway to the land, and not merely a gateway but a gatekeeper. It wielded its authority often to the detriment of small-scale provincial industries like weaving in Catamarca or Córdoba, or textiles, wines and spirits in Mendoza and Catamarca. The competition from excessive foreign imports hit the provinces hard, a phenomenon that would come to the fore in later years.

CRIOLLOS

However, the most important social phenomenon of this period was the emergence of an ambitious class who were taking on ever greater significance, namely the *criollos*. They were born in America, had no mixed blood (at least in their appearance) and were preceded by three, four or even five generations of Spanish stock.

Provinces such as La Rioja or Catamarca were to all intents and purposes (barring the occasional Spanish trader who had been accepted by local society) run by *criollos* on the city council. This reminds us that the shrewd, intricate politics of post-1810 Argentina had its precedent in the *cabildos,* with *criollos* and Spaniards bidding for power. They must have been a training ground in disputes both for the *criollos* and their descendents.

Criollos were energetic men of action, resentful of Spaniards whom they scoffed at or belittled, and had an unshakeable love of the land they had been born in. There exist minutes of a *cabildo* meeting in 1770 odd in Santiago del Estero which describe an exchange over a procedural issue between a Spaniard and a *criollo* by the name of Bravo. The ensuing fight was so heated that Bravo, who apparently lived up to his name (in Spanish *bravo* means 'wild'), is recorded as saying to the Spaniard "May the honourable gentleman respectfully go to hell".

THE ENGLISH INVASIONS

The existence of the *criollo* was a new factor which created pressure in the Viceroyalty. Meanwhile, Buenos Aires as a city was gradually becoming more genteel and could boast an important theatre, a printing press, the Paseo de la Alameda, a viceroyal court which, although on the rough-and-ready side, could plausibly be compared to Lima's or New Spain's. Not bad going for a city in those days.

Between Buenos Aires and the provinces there was, as we have said, a latent antagonism. But, for the moment, this showed no serious signs of turning into open hostility. In a short space of time, the city had taken the initiative. Its newly acquired power and wealth gave it a special status within the Spanish American empire as a model of a new social class and a new type of wealth. As Ricardo Levene has pointed out, these and other factors were an explosive mixture that eventually led to the revolution of 1810.

The English Invasions of 1806 and 1807 were another event linked to the creation of the Viceroyalty which added to the volatility of the situation. This was in fact really one single invasion with the English setting up camp on the Banda Oriental side of the River Plate and from there invading and occupying Buenos Aires. Though they were dislodged from the capital, they held their position on the Uruguayan coast and with reinforcements mounted a fresh attack only to face final defeat with the city's recapture. But what exactly were the immediate effects of the English Invasions on the increasing influence of Buenos Aires, on the friction between it and the provinces, and on the new awareness, which, though it cannot yet be called nationalism, was embodied in the *criollos*?

In the first place, the administrative power of all the jurisdictions in the Viceroyalty was centralised in Buenos Aires. Though the city fell into English hands, it was recaptured and its administrative structures suffered no damage. Cities in the provinces continued paying it due respect.

Secondly, Buenos Aires acquired a new military prestige. Until 1806 Spain had kept a regiment stationed in Buenos Aires called the *Regimiento Fijo* (the Fixed Regiment) whose troops were primarily from La Coruña in Galicia. After a year, the soldiers and officers disappeared, either because they were trading, marrying native women or simply deserting. In practical terms the *Regimiento Fijo* was not a viable option for repelling the English Invasions. Spain had no power to resist an attack. What on the other hand did become quite apparent was Buenos Aires' very own military prowess. The English soldiers were not greenhorns but fighting men of the first order. They had taken on the might of Napoleon but in Buenos Aires they made mistakes and the people's enthusiasm and Liniers' courage won the day.

After the first wave of the invasion, and in preparation for the second, corps of soldiers were armed and uniformed. They elected their commander-in-chief in keeping with an old Spanish military charter. After some infighting with Manuel Belgrano, Cornelio Saavedra was chosen as head of the so-called *Patricios* (Patricians). These bodies of men were formed according to which region their members came from: there were corps from the provinces up north and the "Patricians" from Buenos Aires; there were Galicians, Basques, Catalans, mulattos and negroes.

The corps of Spaniards were generally made up of men of relatively high social standing, most of whom were traders. They had to leave their jobs for the tedious life of the barracks and perform various exercises and manoeuvres. This life did not suit them and they gradually ducked out of their duties. The *criollos,* on the other hand, who were comparatively poor, took to the soldier's life and the salary they were given with great enthusiasm. These corps constituted what today we would call considerable fire power. Moreover, they formed a military force that was virtually independent of the Spanish crown and had its own resources.

Thirdly, after the English Invasions, the fame and reputation of Buenos Aires spread rapidly through the Americas not only for having fought off the invader but also because they had played a leading role in an event unprecedented in Spanish imperial history, namely the overthrow of the King's representative, Rafael de Sobremonte. Sobremonte appeared as little better than a coward in *Porteño* eyes. He had followed to the letter instructions dating back to Cevallos' day. These stated that if there were an attack from abroad, the first duty of the viceroy was to safeguard royal funds along with those of private individuals and to flee, which is precisely what he did.

After the recapture of Buenos Aires, the people screamed for Sobremonte to be overthrown and, in the face of this ill-feeling, the *Audiencia* endorsed the people's decision suspending the Viceroy, despite his protests, and appointing Santiago de Liniers in his stead. Though Liniers was never appointed by the crown, he did in fact become a caretaker of sorts appointed by the people. This set a crucial precedent: the overthrow of the viceroy by the people was something never before witnessed anywhere in the Spanish empire.

To recap briefly then, the Viceroyalty of the River Plate was set up in 1776 to govern a vast jurisdiction that ultimately benefited Buenos Aires. It brought the capital both prosperity and administrative power. After the English Invasions, the city not only strengthened its administrative powers through the loyalty of the smaller provincial cities and its competition with Córdoba, Salta and Montevideo, but also acquired redoubtable military power and great moral prestige. This was what the region looked like on the eve of the May Revolution.

CHAPTER III THE 1810 REVOLUTION AND ITS AFTERMATH

This chapter is about a key event: the 1810 Revolución de Mayo *(May Revolution). Rather than concentrating on the bare facts, I shall deal with its meaning and consequences, the changes that took place in River Plate society, and what new conflicts the May Revolution sparked off in its efforts to face up to old problems, above all its dependence on Spain.*

In retrospect, the 1810 Revolution seems inevitable, the events leading up to such drastic action making it seem an almost foregone conclusion. Having said this, I shall first outline the national background to the period so that the reader can see why Buenos Aires' neighbours took such an outrageous and extreme decision as deposing the king's representative and appointing an Assembly in his place.

A NEW DYNASTY

England and Spain had been at loggerheads since 1804, though in fact hostilities had started at the end of the eighteenth century. Among other reasons, this war was particularly important because the Battle of Trafalgar (1805), when both the Spanish and French fleets were virtually wiped out, was a turning point in the ongoing warfare between Napoleon and the British Empire.

The war between France and England set the scene for the political events in Spain. Charles IV was on the throne, but it was really Charles IV's Prime Minister, Manuel Godoy the Prince of Peace and María Luisa's favourite, who was pulling the strings of power. Manuel Godoy's policy was to back France all the way. England was an enemy to both countries, so it seemed sensible enough that Spain should seek support in Napoleon. However, when the queen's favourite allowed Napoleon's troops to cross Spanish territory in order to attack Portugal, many Spaniards considered Godoy had gone too far in siding with the French. Napoleon, who had a broader conception of the war, was pondering the efficacy of a continental blockade, a kind of pan-European alliance against the English aiming at preventing them from exporting their increasingly important textiles. The alliance's siege would stifle their production and create such economic chaos that it would finally bring them to their knees. One of the key points of the blockade's success was precisely to put an end to Portugal's traditional loyalty to Great Britain.

With the support of the Spanish, the French troops reached Portugal and met with hardly any resistance on their way. As the French were approaching Lisbon, the members of the Portuguese royal family and their courtiers boarded a ship and moved to Rio de Janeiro. The fact that the courtiers of the King of Portugal, his relatives and the entire bureaucracy should settle in Rio de Janeiro was very significant and was to affect the course of events in the River Plate.

Meanwhile in Spain, the pro-French policy continued until the people rose up against Godoy. There was such violent rioting in Aranjuez, where the Spanish monarchs usually spent their summer holidays, that Godoy finally had to resign. Charles IV was forced to abdicate and in March 1808 his son Ferdinand VII came to the throne much to Napoleon's vexation since he would no longer find such pliant instruments in Spain as Godoy and Charles.

As a result, Napoleon had to flex his muscles and summoned the Spanish royal family to Bayonne in May 1808. In a meeting that was nothing but a farce, Napoleon made Ferdinand VII give the crown back to his father, and in turn made Charles hand it over to himself. Napoleon in turn handed it to his brother Joseph Bonaparte, whom he named King of Spain. So in the blink of an eye, Spain witnessed the fall of the Bourbon dynasty and the rise of a usurping commoner dynasty, the Bonapartes. Ferdinand VII was confined to the castle of Talleyrand in Valençay, and Charles IV and his wife retired to Italy with Godoy.

Joseph Bonaparte began ruling Spain in the name of his brother, supported by French battalions and regiments. This triggered an extremely hostile reaction among the Spanish people, who began to rise up from 1808 onwards all over the peninsula; they organised themselves into people's councils and regional councils and sent delegates to a central council.

Then international allegiances changed. Spain had been at war with England and then became her ally against Napoleon. The Bonapartist forces suffered some setbacks in Spain, but after the battle of Wagram in 1809, when Napoleon put an end to his military difficulties with Austria, he sent mass reinforcements to the Iberian peninsula and occupied it almost entirely. The only region that resisted was Andalucía. In its capital Seville, the Central Council, only very recently created, in effect took over the powers of the rest.

In the meantime, there was great unrest in the Viceroyalty of the River Plate, where loyalty to the Bourbon dynasty made the new French dynasty unwelcome. And it so happened that, because of an unfortunate coincidence, the head of the Viceroyalty at the time was a Frenchman by the name of Liniers who had been appointed by the people of Buenos Aires to replace the Marquis of Sobremonte. Liniers may never officially have been appointed viceroy in Spain, but he was accepted provisionally by the Council of Seville anyway until things cooled down. This and the fact that he was French aroused suspicion. To make matters worse, Liniers was not a very shrewd politician and made mistakes more to do with form than content, which only fuelled doubts in the River Plate over what role he was to play.

In addition the Spanish Infanta Carlota, Ferdinand VII's sister and wife of the heir to the throne of Portugal, was with the Portuguese royal family in Rio de Janeiro. Because she was Ferdinand VII's closest sister and he was being held captive at the time, Carlota considered herself in effect entitled to head a kind of protectorate over the Viceroyalty of the River Plate. Her intrigues with the British Empire and her constant encroachment upon domestic affairs in the River Plate undoubtedly made things worse.

The new viceroy sent by the Central Council of Seville arrived in July 1809. He was a Spanish seaman by the name of Baltasar Hidalgo de Cisneros. Heedless of the advice of Carlota's followers, Liniers remained loyal to the crown, handed power over to Cisneros and retired to Córdoba. A few months later, in May 1810, news reached the River Plate that the Bonapartists had occupied Andalucía, where the last people's council in Spain against the French had been holding out. The news caused a tremendous commotion and triggered the events of May: the famous meeting called by the *Cabildo*, with notification to the viceroy, led to the inhabitants' open pronouncement on what was to be done.

REVOLUTION

To recap, Buenos Aires was a viceroyalty that depended on Spain. Regardless of the farce in Bayonne, the legitimate king, Ferdinand VII, was being held prisoner. The people resisted the usurper king Joseph Bonaparte. The people's councils that had fought against the French had been shattered. What was to be done? Surrender to the Bonaparte dynasty? Play along with the usurper who had taken over most of Europe? Wait and see what happened on the battlefields of the Old Continent? These were just some of the questions that troubled *Porteños.*

In May 1810 various sectors of society with different ideas about the fate of Argentina came together. It is likely that some of the participants in the May sessions, such as Mariano Moreno or Juan José Castelli, wanted to rush headlong into independence. Others such as the Spanish or their supporters may have thought it best to create a council and wait and see.

Some people remembered what had happened a century before when the war of succession between the Hapsburgs and the Bourbons lasted almost fifteen years. Throughout that period the colonies had waited to see what Spain's decision would be, and had been willing to acknowledge the rightful king. Once Phillip V, the first Bourbon king, had settled into the Spanish throne, the colonial officials of the Crown acknowledged his legitimacy and things continued without much ado. Many people in 1810 most likely thought the same thing would happen. What in fact happened was that a council was formed to replace the viceroy.

The prestige Buenos Aires had was by now well and truly consolidated. It added a new dimension to the judicial and governmental arena during the May Sessions of 1810. In the 'open' *cabildo* of May 22 one of those advocating no change and keeping the viceroy stated that the residents of Buenos Aires had no right to take such an important initiative as replacing the viceroy with a council. No matter how important Buenos Aires was, it was one of several cities of the Viceroyalty and therefore it seemed reasonable to consult the opinion of the other jurisdictions. It is worth reminding the reader that at that time, the *intendencias* and subordinate cities had a right to state their own point of view.

This was the moment when Juan José Paso, a shrewd and sophisticated politician, appealed to the "big sister" argument. He claimed that, in the face of this emergency, Buenos Aires was acting as an elder sister who takes the assets and interests of her younger siblings into her custody, and that she should naturally commit herself to summoning the delegates from the rest of the cities for them to ratify the decision to replace the viceroy.

That day the rhetorical figure of the eldest sister took on a concrete juridical dimension. Buenos Aires obtained the right to introduce this substantial change in the power structure of the Viceroyalty on condition that she would then summon the other jurisdictions so that they could have their say.

Another equally important concept was launched in the 22 May session: the idea of the sovereignty of the people. One of the legal theories that came up in the debate was that power lies in the crown because it is legitimately given by God. But the following point made was that the crown had been snatched from the rightful king and if the councils themselves had been defeated militarily, with whom did power lie? With the people, who could provisionally delegate it to the person or persons they wished until things got back to normal.

This concept was extremely important. Nowadays it is a commonplace in Political Law but at the time it was revolutionary. The idea that people could choose their own rulers, even if temporarily, was a bombshell.

Criollo power was not only on the increase in the legal arena but had been consolidated in the military sphere as well. It is worth reminding the reader that, after the first English invasion and the recapture of Buenos Aires, a series of military corps were organised according to the regions their members were originally from; there were Galicians, Catalans, *Arribeños* (citizens from the north), Patricians, *mestizos*, blacks, and so on. The Spanish, as has been stated in the previous chapter, were mostly tradesmen and therefore well-off. They considered military exercises a waste of time and money. The native *criollos*, *mestizos* and blacks, however, badly needed the rations and scanty salaries, so they were quick to comply with their duties and this led them to acquire considerable military skills.

THE REVOLUTION IN THE PROVINCES

By 1810 Buenos Aires' military power was firmly established: the pressure from the *criollo* regiments could be clearly felt and expeditions were immediately sent to various points in the Viceroyalty. What had happened in Buenos Aires was in fact too outrageous for it to be accepted peacefully. The overthrow of the king's delegate or the *Junta* that claimed to represent him and its replacement by another *Junta* was very hard to swallow for the loyalist regions in the Viceroyalty of the River Plate.

In Córdoba there was a counter-revolution led by Liniers, who ended up being executed along with his cronies. In Mendoza there was considerable reticence over accepting the *Porteño Junta* and in Salta a heated debate was raging. Resistance became especially active in Alto Perú, Paraguay and Montevideo. The latter had been a long-standing rival of Buenos Aires, and opposition had grown while Liniers was viceroy because he was not acknowledged as such in Montevideo owing to his French origins. A *Junta* was formed that was dissolved upon the arrival of Cisneros, but the germs of an *anti-Porteño* attitude still lingered, so when Buenos Aires appointed the *Junta*, military resistance was organised in Montevideo and kept up for four years.

Expeditionary forces set out from Buenos Aires in several waves. One of them, led by Manuel Belgrano, left for Paraguay to try to bring its inhabitants round to the revolutionary cause. The landlocked Paraguayans had their own concerns to see to and their interests clashed with those of Buenos Aires. The city was their main gateway for exports and imports, and as such they were expected to revere it. Belgrano fought a battle and lost it, then negotiated with the Paraguayans, who finally remained neutral in the ensuing war of independence and abstained from rubbing *Porteño* authorities up the wrong way.

The expedition sent to Alto Perú won its first battle at Suipacha, but after a few months it was badly defeated at Huaqui on the shores of the River Desaguadero, the border between the viceroyalties of the River Plate and Perú.

It was clear that the troops had been sent to seek recognition for the Buenos Aires authorities rather than to extend their power into other viceroyalties. Buenos Aires considered herself an heir to Spanish power only as far as the viceroyal borders.

The expeditions to Alto Perú were later taken over by Manuel Belgrano, who won the battles of Tucumán and Salta and was defeated at Vilcapugio and Ayohuma. Then General José Rondeau took command of the army and reached Alto Perú's hinterland, where he was defeated in Sipe Sipe in 1815. After that no more expeditions were sent from Buenos Aires. But instead permanent guerrilla warfare was encouraged by the *caudillo,* Martín Miguel de Güemes, who managed to put a stop to the royalists' advance further south. *Caudillos* were tough leaders who fought for self-government of their region.

The other source of military trouble was Montevideo which assigned a fleet to harass Buenos Aires. The Orientals, as the Uruguayans were known in those days, even bombarded the city and raided towns along the Paraná river. Spanish resistance in Montevideo underwent various changes: the royalists were besieged there and José G. Artigas, who had been chosen by the people of the Banda Oriental as their *caudillo*, took part in the fight for independence by supporting the *Porteño Junta*, but then disagreed with its members and withdrew in 1814. Nevertheless, the 'national' troops managed to take Montevideo and this allowed José de San Martín to change his military strategy for the Revolution and put into action his planned expeditions to Chile and Perú.

Equally important were the events triggered off in Buenos Aires and the provinces by the viceroy being replaced with a government that was starting to bandy about the word 'national'. Naturally, there were several wings ranging from the more radical ones represented by Mariano Moreno and Juan José Castelli to the more conservative, led by Saavedra. Likewise, there were several factions that succeeded one another in power between 1810 and 1820 when the central government fell.

However, the fact is that throughout those ten years there was a government which, regardless of the various legal forms, regulations and names it adopted such as First *Junta*, Great *Junta*, Triumvirate, Second Triumvirate or Directoire, did have a base in the city, regarded itself as heir to Spanish power, collected money mainly from the customs and broadly speaking allotted it to the national cause of Independence (in other words, arming and clothing the national armies, sending diplomats abroad to spread the revolutionary word, and so on). Despite its downfall in 1820, the Directoire had all the attributes of a central government and over the decade it brought about salient changes in the society of those days, which had begun to call itself 'Argentine'.

CHANGES

In the first place, change was mainly reflected in the collective beliefs of the day. The Common Good was one of the fundamental concepts of Spanish Law in South and Central America. The principle of the common good meant that the measures applied by the State (i.e. the crown, the viceroy or the governor) had to be directed towards the benefit of all. Such a notion accounts for the reason why an order or royal letters patent signed by the king was on occasion acknowledged yet left null and void if the viceroy thought its application in the New World would do more harm than good.

The concept of the common good was discarded after 1810 and replaced by the idea of the sovereignty of the people, one of the banners chosen by theoreticians of the *Revolución de Mayo* such as

Moreno, Castelli and Monteagudo. Although this revolutionary concept would take a whole century to manifest itself in elections, it had nevertheless already been adopted by this new society.

The concept of the sovereignty of the people, which meant that the people could appoint their representatives when there was no legitimate authority, was replaced by Rousseau's thesis that it is the majority that presides, at least in theory, over various elections, appointments and assemblies. Naturally, the change took place gradually but the concept caught on and was nurtured by the measures the government took and the ideas promulgated by political leaders. The fact remains that the changes were geared to achieving a democratic republican society.

Secondly, the population was hit by the disintegration of the Viceroyalty. The Viceroyalty had been conceived in the hope of its becoming a great country; indeed, four present-day nations were later to be born from this vast jurisdiction. Yet precisely, it turned out that the Viceroyalty's fatal flaw was the huge expanse it covered, with its conflicting climate, production, people, customs and interests. Thirty years was too short a period for such incompatible elements to merge and develop into one nation.

By 1810, resistance against the *Revolución de Mayo* mainly centred on Alto Perú, Paraguay, and Montevideo, which favoured secession from the Viceroyalty. This process took about twenty years, but there was no turning back. Alto Perú, which had been placed under the jurisdiction of Buenos Aires in 1776, continued to keep its close bond with Perú and a marked distance from Buenos Aires. There, resistance to 'national' troops was authentic and even popular, and it was the last region in South America remain loyal to the Spanish until the royalists were defeated in the 1824 battle of Ayacucho fought by Simón Bolívar's troops sent from the north and not by *Porteños*. Today's Bolivian national hero, Simón Bolívar, was giving a clear sign that he would protect the new path to independence in those regions. This is how Bolivia was born.

Independence in Paraguay took a few more years and came as late as 1846. After suffering constant, systematic harassment by the Portuguese from 1815 on, the Banda Oriental became the arena of a war between the Argentine Republic and the Brazilian empire, ending in 1827 with the Banda Oriental's declaration of independence. Henceforward, it has been known as the República Oriental del Uruguay.

Once Spanish rule came to an end once and for all, these disintegrating factors were set into motion and the irresistible revolutionary force gradually carved up the regions.

MILITARY MATTERS

In 1810 military needs were to come to the fore. Buenos Aires, a city of shopkeepers and tradesmen, that had deemed it necessary to train battalions and regiments after the English Invasions, soon brought military effort to bear on the revolutionary cause. Indeed, it was Buenos Aires that was carrying out the revolution. There was reticence, resistance and delaying tactics where the provinces' co-operation with the cause was concerned. Then the smaller jurisdictions, such as the *intendencias* (though not the provincial capitals) gradually began to accept or acknowledge the authority of the *Junta* and their towns and cities followed suit.

However, on account of the rather rigid and traditional nature of society in the provinces, the new ideas spreading from Buenos Aires took time to catch on, so that most of the burden was mainly born by Buenos Aires. Even though in Córdoba and Tucumán mothers sent their sons to become members of the 'national' armies, the real revolutionary vigour came from Buenos Aires.

Because of this new need for military power, Buenos Aires attributed the utmost importance to everything concerning the military: uniforms, a certain jargon, a style and a value it had never had before. These changes took place especially after 1812 when the first professional military men, José de San Martín and Carlos de Alvear, appeared on the scene to serve the revolutionary cause. The previous leaders, such as Manuel Belgrano, a lawyer, had been appointed generals simply because there was no one else who fitted the bill. Miguel de Azcuénaga had been the only brigadier, and not a very efficient one at that.

San Martín and Alvear began to urge young men from the higher classes to join the army as officers so after a while being in the military became the height of fashion. The sons of household names in high society such as the Escaladas, the Balcarces and the like, took up training as officers as a serious profession, for a war which was also to be long and hard.

The militarising of society altered the basis of the traditional order. José María Paz, who served in practically every 'national' army that existed after 1813, wrote in his memoirs that he could not remember a single horse ever being bought; when they were needed they were to be had for nothing. At best, the horse's owner was given a token voucher in exchange. This was remarkably different from the previous order, under which private property was respected and protected by the Spanish authorities.

The new state of affairs fostered the emergence of military *caudillos*. These were born into a society which delegated a certain share of its assets to arms-bearing leaders who were to defend the revolution and some of these *caudillos* would later become sabre-rattling tyrants.

Another interesting new development was the birth of anti-Spanish feeling. After 1810 when the severing of links with Spain became more apparent (although Ferdinand VII had returned to the throne, the Revolution was well underway by then) enmity towards everything Spanish pervaded all walks of life. Spaniards became the enemy and showing one's hostility towards them was compulsory. This feeling was reflected in a vast number of areas, one of which was literature. Although the Romantic movement would take a few more years to cross the Atlantic, Hispanic arts and classical forms were already far from welcome.

In some cases this rejection was reflected in very specific measures. For example, the First *Junta* ordered that all Spanish bachelors be expelled from Buenos Aires. This caused a terrible mess: courtships were broken off and families destroyed, so much so that much lobbying went on with the *Junta* for it to repeal the measure. Then, as often happens in Argentina, the text of the first decree was enlarged by another exempting bachelors who could prove their solidarity with the

Revolution with references and the like. In the end, the measure was annulled.

The reader may be wondering how come there was such widespread antagonism against Spaniards if ninety-five percent of the population was Spanish or first generation. Personally, I believe this society needed some form of identity and in achieving it, it had to rebel against its father and persuade itself that he had been tyrannical, despotic and mean. This is quite an understandable mechanism.

The *criollo* sons' and daughters' spirit of rebellion against their Spanish fathers and grandfathers was quite remarkable. An English traveller by the name of Brackenridge wrote in 1810 that along the fashionable *paseo* in Buenos Aires called the Alameda, he noticed ghostly groups of men in shabby attire who spoke in melancholy tones to one another; these were Spaniards who had been rich tradesmen and respectable citizens of Buenos Aires but who had been cast out by the revolution and lived in poverty now that the chain linking the tradesmen and shopkeepers of Buenos Aires to those of Cádiz had been broken.

Among the many forms this anti-Spanish feeling took, were measures taken against those who were regarded as potential enemies. Martín de Alzaga's conspiracy of 1812 showed that this feeling had reached its peak. Alzaga was shot and his assets expropriated for having been the leader of what could have been a really dangerous revolutionary uprising mostly funded or led by old, rich Spaniards whose power had waned.

Such maltreatment was dished out to Spanish prisoners as well. Unlike the battle of Salta, where Belgrano signed an agreement with the Spanish general for all Spanish prisoners to be set free, in the battle of Tucumán a large number were confined to certain cities in the Viceroyalty. Most of them stayed there. In fact, I myself am a descendant of a Spaniard who was taken prisoner in Tucumán. His name was Tomás Valdés and he later settled in La Rioja, married, and died many years later as a respected local figure.

General San Martín sent many prisoners to Mendoza to work for *criollo* owners instead of being sold into what amounted to slavery, as the slaves had been summoned to fight for the 'national' armies. In other cases, some Spaniards were treated even more harshly; for several years there was a 'concentration camp' near Dolores called Las Bruscas, where Spanish prisoners were very cruelly treated. There are a number of memoirs written by the prisoners denouncing their living conditions, the weather and the food. Some of them even tried to break out.

A very respectable citizen of Mendoza, Don Faustino Ansái, for example, led a very hazardous life, which he wrote about in his fascinating memoirs. In 1810 he was one of the leaders of the group that refused to recognise the authority of the Buenos Aires Council. He was defeated in the *cabildo*, arrested and sent as a prisoner to Las Bruscas, which was only just beginning to operate. Ansái fled and took refuge in Montevideo. When the 'national' armies seized the city, he was caught and sent back to Las Bruscas, and only regained his freedom in 1820.

Anti-Spanish feeling also altered the *Porteño* life-style. The short *calzón* (knee-breeches), typical of well-to-do Spaniards, gradually fell out of favour and was replaced by trousers brought by American soldiers. There are portraits of Mariano Moreno wearing a short *calzón* and white socks, and in his famous honours decree he himself spoke of having to wear a tail-coat in order to be admitted to official ceremonies. These forms of attire, the bow and pompous Spanish etiquette were soon put aside in favour of the simple Anglo-Saxon handshake. Similarly, chocolate was replaced by tea.

These cultural changes were also brought about by the fact that, along with free trade brought in by the new Council, an English colony and a smaller group of Frenchmen gradually settled in. The 'national' authorities had an overall liberal attitude in the commercial arena. There were no restrictions whatsoever. Anybody could import any kind of merchandise as long as they paid their duties. They could also buy and export goods. This policy was not the result of liberal thinking but a necessity in times of war and insofar as there was plenty of trade going on and duties were being paid, the large sums collected allowed the government of Buenos Aires to arm, feed, and clothe its 'national' armies.

Hence, English tradesmen began to settle in Buenos Aires. As a result of Napoleon's wars and the European blockade, England soon found it was overstocked with merchandise for which it was hard to find a buyer. Seeking out new markets, many English traders travelled to Buenos Aires because even before 1810, the viceroy Cisneros had authorised a certain degree of openness in the markets. This meant that, apart from English tradesmen settling in the city, many of them travelled the country seeking new and advantageous marketing opportunities. At the same time, they brought their customs, their style and language. While the provinces maintained a more conservative stance, Buenos Aires was a window on the outside world.

Commercial liberalisation and the war had a number of effects. Since most of Alto Perú was under the power of the Spanish, the traditional trade in mules in the colonial era had come to a standstill, and with it the inflow of monies in circulation from the region. Previously, the miners of Alto Perú had travelled to Salta, where they bought mules and paid for them in cash; the local muleteers and producers packed their silver coins into bags. But the war put an end to trade and money became scarce.

Besides, the English tradesmen demanded that their goods be paid for in hard currency, especially silver and this also contributed to the dearth. They mainly carried good, cheap woollens and cloths of better quality than were found in Argentina; household goods, knives, pots and pans and any other merchandise they could sell quickly. Furniture was mainly brought over by the Americans. These sales had to be paid in hard currency by the population of the old Viceroyalty, so after some years money began to be scarce, causing a number of financial difficulties.

TOWARDS A KIND OF DEMOCRACY

One of the new ideas the *Revolución* brought with it was the notion of equality, that there should be no privileges, that all citizens were equal. At the time it was still a very abstract idea but later it was to take root in Argentine society and acquire a more tangible expression in the following decades. The anti-Spanish feeling, the liberalisation of trade, the concepts of the sovereignty of the people and equality were all changes that involved a transformation that was as direct and abrupt as the *Revolución de Mayo* had been.

Apart from these, there are two other factors which were of some importance. During the *Revolución* the seeds of something one might call 'public opinion' were sown and spread in the newspapers in editorials and critical articles such as those written by Mariano Moreno. For the first time, the newspapers (instead of publishing the usual dull business news, the odd scientific breakthrough or some European upheaval, as they had done in the days of the Viceroyalty) brought under discussion revolutionary, stimulating and often shocking ideas for a public that was only just awakening to this type of debate.

Elections were another novelty. Every time Buenos Aires summoned a representative body such as the 1813 Constituent Assembly or the 1816 Congress in Tucumán, people gathered in every city of the old Viceroyalty and appointed someone to represent them in Buenos Aires before the official bodies. Obviously, the people who met were the same class of citizens who would have taken part in the open *cabildos* during colonial times and were dubbed 'the healthiest and principal part' of society. They were formed by the residents who had a respectable house, family and job. But the masses still had no vote.

Slaves and *mestizos* did not vote, neither did white citizens regardless of whether they were Spanish or *criollo*, unless they had a respectable trade. Butchers and shoemongers did not vote. Suffrage was therefore restricted to an elite who had never before exercised the duties of meeting, setting up a *cabildo*, electing, taking the minutes, signing them or even passing on instructions.

There was a movement going on in public opinion; the public arena was alive with thought, imagination and persuasion and this was reflected in the press, in restricted elections and in the various avatars of 'national' governments from the *Junta* to the Directoire, in military events, and in the opening of trade that linked this part of America to the rest of the world. Between 1810 and 1820 the *Revolución de Mayo* underwent a sea change. Entirely new events took place, there was a real transformation of society whose expressions took on a freer, more self-assured and even youthful tone. These were the circumstances that were to foster several revolutionary leaders who would have had no opportunity whatsoever of becoming politically prominent under old-style colonialism.

CHAPTER IV THE SEARCH FOR A POLITICAL FORMULA

When a nation embarks upon a new stage in its development there are a number of questions it asks itself either explicitly or implicitly. For Argentines in 1810, the first such question was what kind of relationship they would now have with the mother country. There were those who thought it was not worthwhile getting embroiled in an out-and-out confrontation for independence, believing instead that it was best to establish a kind of commonwealth with Spain. However, the very dynamics of the war rendered this impossible. Besides, when Ferdinand VII returned to the throne in 1815, an absolutist policy was imposed which ran contrary to the liberal ideas in Buenos Aires at the time.

The second important question was what political system the new United Provinces of the River Plate would be given. One possible model was the United States. Thirty years earlier the English colonies in North America had declared their independence, passed a constitution and set a truly new political system in motion, namely, the democratic republic, at a time (the end of the eighteenth century) when the progressive choice seemed to be a constitutional monarchy. Having broken free from their mother country, the English settlers chose the republican system. This existed nowhere else at the time, though it had been in use two thousand years earlier in Greece and Rome.

Republican feeling had also been present in the Viceroyalty of the River Plate. The natural temperament of its inhabitants, their free lifestyle, rural work habits, the vast distances, everything seemed to point to a future republican and even federal, political model. However, in these latitudes there was also a centralist tradition, which had been strengthened during the Viceroyalty with Buenos Aires' ascendancy as capital. It is as well to point out that the gobernaciones-intendencias, *or province-townhall authorities, (for example, Córdoba and Salta on present-day Argentine territory and others in Alto Perú and Paraguay) were under the jurisdiction of Buenos Aires, and that there were subordinate towns in constant rivalry with the main ones.*

LEGAL INNOVATIONS

Regarding the question posed from 1810 onwards of what political system to apply, (republic, monarchy, federal republic, or centralist republic?) the discussions during the *Jornadas de Mayo* (May Sessions) were not only based on the experience of the *cabildos,* the province-town hall authorities and viceroyal centralism, but also on two legal principles that were, politically speaking, to become very significant in the years to come. These were the doctrines of 'retroversion' and 'subrogation'.

The *Junta* sworn in in May 1810 to substitute the viceroy subrogated in effect all his powers and functions. The fact is that in spite of the huge differences in political terms between viceroyalty and independence, the members of this *Junta* and of the subsequent governments (the Great *Junta*, the First Triumvirate, the Second Triumvirate and the Directoire) considered themselves entitled to all the powers the viceroy had possessed and as a result aspired to ruling the land.

Buenos Aires justified its centralism over the rest of viceroyal territory after 1810 by brandishing the concept of 'subrogation'. This is why, for example, the first expedition sent from the Viceroyalty of the River Plate to Alto Perú in June 1810 was ordered to halt at the Desaguadero river separating the two jurisdictions: if the *Junta de Mayo* was subrogated to the viceroy's authority, they were not entitled to go beyond the viceroy's former jurisdiction.

The other doctrine, 'retroversion', consisted of the people's right to choose their own authorities in the event that legitimate authority should for whatever reason cease. This was the case in 1810 when the legitimate king Ferdinand VII was being held a prisoner and the Central Council of Seville, the highest authority in Spain at the time, were believed to be under arrest from the French.

This theory was eagerly adopted by many lawyers from Buenos Aires and the provinces, where it rapidly became popular. The inhabitants of Jujuy, for instance, who wanted self-government, appealed to the principle in order to deny Salta the power to send them governors. These federal sentiments gradually took hold throughout the viceroyalty and were to flare up after 1820.

The way the concepts of retroversion and subrogation caught on among the people is an example of the fact that legal theories are not merely abstract, but can sometimes take root, acquire a life of their own and rapidly spread to the political arena.

BUENOS AIRES AND THE PROVINCES

From the moment the First *Junta* took over the rights and powers of the viceroy, tension began to mount between Buenos Aires and the provinces. The city not only aspired to carry on managing government, but also to appointing governor-mayors, sending armies to enforce their recognition, establishing diplomatic relations with other countries and, of course, collecting taxes, which mainly amounted to customs duties. Revenues were generally allotted to defraying expenses from the newly-formed independent army, the public service, propaganda in the revolutionary cause and diplomatic representations.

Meanwhile in the provinces there was a rapidly growing feeling that the May Revolution had merely replaced the despotism of Madrid with the tyranny of Buenos Aires. The bitterest resentment came from Lima, the royalists' stronghold, though being so far away it posed no real threat. Within the Viceroyalty of the River Plate, rivalry had always been more intense with the Banda Oriental, since Montevideo had always aspired to being the gateway to this part of America herself on account of having the better port.

The centralist *Porteño* regime began to be seriously questioned both by the royalist majority in Montevideo at the time, and by the inhabitants of the surrounding countryside, who were mainly represented by the *caudillo* José G. Artigas, a mulish man of obvious popularity and charisma and the occasional bright idea, who had a knowledge of American federalism. The disagreements surfaced in the 1813 Assembly to which Artigas sent delegates with proposals that were rejected. He consequently sent no delegates to the Congress of Tucumán.

Artigas' political thinking and military action not only affected the Banda Oriental, but also the littoral provinces (Entre Ríos, Corrientes, Santa Fe) and at one time Córdoba as well. His stand was significant in several ways. In the first place, he had enough power to deprive the real jurisdiction of Buenos Aires of a large part of the former viceroyalty, and secondly, his dissent was based on a clear political stance inspired by the United States.

One could question whether Artigas' policy at the time was right, on the basis that circumstances here were different to those in the United States. For example, in the former American colonies there were governors usually sent by the British crown and ruling on an equal footing with local legislatures, whose members were prominent citizens. This meant that they had had some experience of pseudo-democratic rule. Moreover, the structure of the American population consisted of small towns and cities, in which usually literate people had some knowledge of public opinion through reading local newspapers. This was the scenario of the American revolution which had laid the foundations for democracy by the time Washington became President.

In Argentina however, the case was quite different. Cities were thin on the ground and hundreds of miles apart. There was no public opinion and the majority of the population was illiterate. Nor did the necessary conditions exist for the development of political parties as in the United States, which has led to present-day American democracy, hence the enormous difficulties involved in establishing a power structure that could meet the standards of some rudimentary form of democracy.

Artigas was nevertheless expressing a localist feeling worth bearing in mind. This sentiment was part of his reaction against Buenos Aires centralism, which admittedly did sometimes get out of hand, but was also partly due to unique regional traits. It should be remembered that the former viceroyalty was made up of widely differing territories: Alto Perú and Paraguay had nothing in common, nor did the present-day Northwest and Buenos Aires. Ethnic composition, landscape, production, regional character were all different and each region had its own rivalries and loyalties and an understandable localist feeling that was eventually embodied in the figure of the *caudillo*.

From the May Revolution onwards federalist feelings grew more intense and spread through all the Argentine provinces mainly at Artigas' instigation. This federalist sentiment was quite unique: whereas law and order were respected in the former British colonies in America, from the very first settlements in the mid-sixteenth century Argentina's colonial past was plagued with uproar, mutiny, sedition and struggles against the authorities, who were regarded as authoritarian or tyrannical. For example, the second governor of Tucumán, Jerónimo Luis de Cabrera, was beheaded by his successor Gonzalo de Abreu, who was in his turn beheaded by his successor Hernando de Lerma. There was no such tradition in the United States, which makes American political struggles look rather mild when compared to Argentine ones.

In 1815 the first national revolution against central power took place: a general rebellion against the appointment of Carlos María de Alvear as Supreme Director. As a result, he was deposed two or three months later. In fact, as early as 1812, the First Triumvirate had been overthrown and the Second Triumvirate set up, a move to which both San Martín and Alvear had tacitly agreed. On 5 April 1811 the Great *Junta* presided over by Saavedra had been strengthened by a people's movement, and this shows that misgivings about the central power tended to be solved not only by way of reasoning and debate but also by taking up arms.

INDEPENDENCE

In 1815 a violent change of government took place. The Revolution was going through a bad spell in the political and military arenas and was badly in need of an infusion of new fervour. In the political arena, Ferdinand VII returned to the throne that year. In the military arena, after the defeat at Sipe Sipe, troops from the Alto Perú auxiliary force had to retreat almost as far as Salta. Paraguay remained neutral, and although they had taken Montevideo (the great victory of 1814), all the revolutionary movements allied to the one in Buenos Aires had been quashed.

The need to declare independence became urgent and, even though it was not an issue that had been explicitly mentioned, this was the direction the country had been steering itself in since the times of the Viceroyalty. After the 1813 Assembly, Argentina had a flag, a national anthem and a currency. There were substantive laws establishing the freedom of the press, abolishing slavery for anyone yet to be born, annulling the titles and primogeniture of the nobility, and outlawing the black slave trade. However, it was necessary for the reality to be sanctioned with a formal declaration of independence, and this took place on 9 July 1816 in Tucumán.

Once the question of independence was settled, another important issue was what form of government to choose and the Congress in Tucumán seriously considered making the country a monarchy. Napoleon had been defeated and the Holy Alliance of Czarist Russia, Prussia and Austria under Metternich was in the ascendant. In this context, a republican system smacked of subversion, chaos, Jacobinism.

Some prominent citizens like Manuel Belgrano recommended monarchy and the proposal was to an extent put into practice, although this entailed complex diplomatic negotiations in Europe. There was also talk of restoring a native Inca to the throne. However, these choices never went further than probing public opinion, which, hazy as it may have been, repudiated the sole idea of a monarch in Buenos Aires and preferred a freer, more democratic form. It would, besides, have spelt the end of the road for the Revolution, and so the setting up of a monarchy was ruled out and Independence declared. The Congress of Tucumán moved to Buenos Aires and continued to hold its sessions there in order to draw up a Constitution. This was the Constitution of 1819, which was written with a possible monarchy in mind and therefore never practically enforced. It showed aristocratic leanings, with a Senate made up of delegates from the provinces and other distinguished members of society such as university heads, generals, bishops, and the like. The word 'republic' was never mentioned in the text. The 1819 Constitution never worked because of strong federalist dissent and a deep distrust of royal machinations. In the meantime General José de San Martín was fighting to liberate Chile.

INFORMAL ORGANISATION

On 1 February 1820 at Cepeda near San Nicolás, two real *caudillos*, Estanislao López and Francisco 'Pancho' Ramírez defeated the remains of the National Army. The event has come to be known as the Battle of Cepeda.

Summoned by the Directoire to fight the *caudillos*, the army from Alto Perú had a few weeks earlier revolted in Arequito. Refusing to fight their fellow citizens the soldiers had retreated to Córdoba thus leaving the Directoire defenceless. The Battle of Cepeda marks the unofficial yet deliberate establishment of a federalist system. Current historiography refers to 1820 as the year of anarchy, from the Greek *an-arkhos* meaning 'without a head', and with the fall of the Directoire and the Congress after the Battle of Cepeda the country was indeed decapitated. From 1810 onwards there had been a government in Buenos Aires that possessed authority on a national scale and whose powers had subrogated those of the former viceroy. From Cepeda onwards, Buenos Aires became just another province: elections were held to vote in a Legislature which, in turn, chose a governor.

During 1820 Buenos Aires underwent a series of political ups and downs including the famous day of the three governors, and it was only towards the end of that year that the political skies cleared. In the same year, thirteen provinces were born, the true basis of the modern nation. There were thirteen of them at the time and not fourteen, as Salta and Jujuy did not separate until 1833.

The new foundation of the provinces meant first and foremost that, after the Battle of Cepeda, López and Ramírez did not impose such harsh conditions on Buenos Aires, but simply requested that a treaty be signed laying down what they considered to be two important principles: nationality and federalism.

The principle of nationality mainly consisted in expressing the idea that the old viceroyalty wished to become a fully-fledged country, a nation. Even though it was undergoing a period of anarchy and upheaval, when the circumstances were ripe it would do just that.

The Treaty of Pilar rather optimistically ruled that within sixty days of being signed a congress would meet at the Convent of San

Lorenzo near Santa Fe, where San Martín had won his first battle, to lay down the foundations for a federal system. Although events interfered with the deadline, the Treaty of Pilar remained as proof of the provinces' will to become a nation.

The second principle that López and Ramírez wanted Buenos Aires to recognise was federalism. The nation was not to be a monarchy, but a federal republic; in other words, a republic in which some authority would be delegated to a central power but each of the provinces would be self-ruled. This was in fact a long-standing tradition dating back to colonial times.

As explained above, the cities of Córdoba and Salta were the seats of the *gobernaciones-intendencias* that other dependent cities looked to for jurisdiction. Córdoba, for instance, had authority over La Rioja, San Luis, Mendoza and San Juan. The truth of the matter was that the subordinate cities abhorred the *gobernaciones-intendencias* because they felt plundered and abused by them, and often sought help from Buenos Aires to alleviate the alleged tyranny. This happened whenever they had financial difficulties such as levying taxes. On being sent delegate governors or lieutenant governors, the dependent cities would appeal to Buenos Aires, which in turn confronted the authorities of the *gobernaciones-intendencias* in question and then bypassed them. Regardless of whether they were dependent or not, it was the *cabildos* in every town and city that kept up the pressure against the *gobernaciones-intendencias*' abusive taxation, and it was the *cabildos* that gradually came to form the core of the federal system that would develop in later years.

When in 1820 the national authorities collapsed and Buenos Aires could no longer appoint administrators to the *gobernaciones-intendencias*, the former *cabildos* turned their regions into provinces: legislatures and governors were appointed; in some cases constitutions were written and in others fiscal regimes established.

Meanwhile, the governor of Córdoba, Juan Bautista Bustos, who had served in the army during the war of independence, had come to power by staging a revolution backed by the Alto Perú army, which had revolted at Arequito a few days before the Battle of Cepeda. Bustos was concerned about the fact that there were several provinces with no prospect of being ruled as they should be in his view. Although he was a supporter of federalism, he believed that the provinces should be modelled on the former *gobernaciones-intendencias* and began to realise that many of them could not afford minimum requirements for self-government, or maintain respectable men of authority, or even a clergy to represent them.

Governor Bustos would obviously have wanted his new province to include Córdoba, San Luis, La Rioja and Cuyo, but the provinces organised on the *cabildo* system wanted to be autonomous, in spite of the fact that several of them had scant resources. Let us take the province of La Rioja in 1820 as an example. What sources of income did it have? Low taxes levied on any cattle, troops or merchandise going through their territory, and a municipal tax collected from licenses to open tap-rooms. These provinces had no fiscal system and were extremely poor, a scenario which over the years grew even worse. However, the claims of the provinces were born of an understandable localist feeling and had somehow to be satisfied.

During the early 1820s Buenos Aires felt ousted from its role as 'elder sister' and seat of national government. It no longer had nationwide obligations. Any customs duties levied were earmarked exclusively for its own needs, such as improving the state of the roads, creating a university and generally instituting everything the progressive leader Bernardino Rivadavia has become famous for. The money that had hitherto been spent on armies and diplomatic missions was now allocated to local needs, whereas in the rest of the provinces the lack of resources drove them to failure, frustration, minor revolutions, riots and so on.

On the one hand Buenos Aires was undergoing what was then called "the joyful experience" of a peace-loving government that submitted its budget to the Legislature year in year out, gave proper account of its expenses, set up new institutions, improved its citizens' standard of living, and took the necessary measure for trade to flourish. However, the situation of the provinces did not improve with Independence at all, but instead deteriorated. After the Battle of Ayacucho in 1824, the last battle of Independence, the region comprising Salta, Jujuy and Tucumán, which had lived off its trade with Alto Perú, was running short of currency and, worse still, had been left without a market to trade its goods on. The Cuyo region was another case in point, although the liberation of Chile did allow it to expand its economic activities a little. Other inland provinces that had no resources of their own went through very hard times.

This is why the need to find some form of constitutional organisation for the country grew more pressing. The provinces were demanding a constitution and Buenos Aires turned a deaf ear to their claims. It was well aware that any such constitution would once again involve a central government it would have to bow to.

WAR WITH BRAZIL

These antagonisms could have gone on indefinitely had it not been for another event that made a constitutional form of organisation necessary: war with Brazil. Although the Banda Oriental had been under the thrall of Artigas, the Portuguese had always had their eyes on it and had begun a slow but steady invasion ending in 1820 with their occupation of Montevideo. A year later, the Banda Oriental was declared a province of the Portuguese Empire, and after Brazilian independence, a province of the Brazilian Empire, and this was considered unacceptable.

The Banda Oriental had always belonged to the Spanish crown and one of the legal notions that was rescued and upheld by the governments after the declaration of independence was that the new nations would keep the same borders as the old colonial jurisdiction. For example, one of the northern borders of the Viceroyalty of the River Plate was the Desaguadero river in Perú, yet when Bolivia became independent it never made any attempt to push its borders beyond this river. Likewise, the Banda Oriental had always belonged to the Spanish crown, hence its occupation by the Portuguese was out-and-out encroachment.

The *Porteño* ruling class realised it was necessary to try and avoid the invasion, and therefore called on all of the provinces to send representatives to a congress that met in Buenos Aires in 1824. After a series of fruitless negotiations with the emperor of Brazil and under pressure from the *Treinta y Tres Orientales* expeditionary force leading the Uruguayan liberation crusade, the government of Buenos Aires declared war on Brazil in the name of all the provinces.

In a sense, the convergence of representatives from every province on the 1824 congress in Buenos Aires spurred the Argentine Republic, as it was by then known, to do its utmost to drive the Brazilians out of the Banda Oriental.

Nevertheless, the congress had a clear Unitarian bias. The provinces had sent their delegates to approve a federal constitution, but the one passed was Unitarian and Bernardino Rivadavia, head of the so-called Unitarians, was elected President. The arrangement did not last long.

The war with Brazil ended on a relatively even footing: Argentina and Uruguay won the land campaign at Ituzaingó, but the blockade imposed on the United Provinces of the River Plate by Brazil was extremely harsh and throttled their economy. A peace treaty was signed whereby the Banda Oriental became an independent republic called the *República Oriental del Uruguay*. The old Viceroyalty fell apart: Bolivia had declared its independence with the consent of the congress, and Paraguay continued to remain neutral and isolated.

From then on the borders of what was later to become the Argentine Republic were fixed but the war with Brazil and Rivadavia's utopian endeavours put an end to his presidency: the Unitarian experiment was foiled by the president's resignation and the country returned to its previous state, namely, thirteen self-governing provinces that entrusted Buenos Aires with their foreign affairs.

Since Buenos Aires had been the viceroyal capital and had the necessary administrative resources, the provinces recognised its capacity for diplomatic relations with the rest of the world. In fact from 1822 onwards, the world's leading nations acknowledged the existence of the *Provincias Unidas del Río de la Plata* as an independent country. The government of Buenos Aires Province thus took on a dual responsibility: seeing to foreign affairs and heeding the provinces inexorable will to become one nation, as they had made clear in the Treaty of Pilar.

CIVIL WAR

Unfortunately, Manuel Dorrego, the Federal governor of Buenos Aires, whom the provincial *caudillos* trusted, was overthrown by a corps of Brazil war veterans led by Juan Lavalle. This event sparked off another period of civil war which was fought in both Buenos Aires and the provinces.

The campaign commander in Buenos Aires, Juan Manuel de Rosas, shouldered the responsibility of resisting those who had staged the coup against Dorrego. After a few battles and some rather muddled encounters, an agreement was reached with Lavalle that Rosas would be the governor of Buenos Aires, and the Legislature that had ruled with Dorrego was reinstated and peace restored.

In the provinces, however, a Unitarian league was formed which unseated the Federal governments. José María Paz was sent to Córdoba, where he immediately overthrew its governor, Bustos, and seized power. Although the league called itself 'Unitarian', what actually united it was its opposition to Rosas rather than any consistent Unitarian ideology. The league clashed with the authorities in Buenos Aires, and this gave rise to the 1831 Federal Pact.

The Pact was an agreement between Buenos Aires, Santa Fe and Corrientes. Its aim was to make an offensive-defensive commitment whereby anyone who attacked one of them would have to take on all three. In addition, it included a commitment to organise the country under the federal system once peace was restored.

When the Federal Pact was signed, a representative from Corrientes, Pedro Ferré, suggested that the new country needed an economic plan. Would it continue to embrace free trade and allow all foreign goods into the country thus forcing the local entrepreneurs into utter poverty? Ferré owned a small shipyard and was well aware of the problems of unbridled free trade and its effects on the provinces' economies after 1810, when the various post-Independence governments had opened up the markets to obtain revenue from customs duties in order to cover their expenses.

Free-trade policies had led to dumping and saturation, especially by the British, and to the annihilation of the handful of local handicraft industries in the provinces, and this led to a drainage on currency and serious shortages. Ferré was requesting that before signing the treaty the parties come to an agreement whereby the local industries (wines, wheat, leather goods) were protected by raising customs duties.

Buenos Aires under Rosas was against this proposal so the Federal Pact was finally signed in January 1831 with no reference whatsoever to an economic policy. The only thing it mentioned was that a commission would be formed representing the three governments and signatories and that, when there was peace, the other provinces would be invited to participate fully.

But at that very moment, the Federal Pact stood for a military power set up against the Unitarian league led by General Paz. The civil war ended that year with Paz being imprisoned following his capture by a soldier from the enemy lines who had accidentally lassoed himwith his *bolas*. With Paz's army defeated, the rest of the Unitarian forces in the provinces were routed by general Juan Facundo Quiroga.

THE LETTER FROM FIGUEROA RANCH

In terms of the Republic's quest for a suitable political structure, another important document was signed in 1834 which, along with the Federal Pact, would become the backbone of the broadly pragmatic form of organisation that sustained the country until the Battle of Caseros.

After his agreement with Lavalle, Rosas held the governorship of Buenos Aires from 1829 to 1831. He ruled befittingly, established a certain degree of order and put an end to the civil war in his province.

After his conquest of the desert, he refused to continue being governor since he wanted to exercise office only with extraordinary powers. In his opinion, things could not be kept in hand unless the governor was a dictator. As the Legislature refused to grant him these powers, Rosas did not accept his re-election and, after his stint, there was a succession of governors, none of whom saw out their terms.

Finally in 1834 news reached Buenos Aires that a civil war had broken out between Tucumán and Salta. Rosas summoned Juan Facundo Quiroga, the most prestigious provincial of his day, who was living in Buenos Aires at the time, and sent him on a peace mission as a representative of provincial authority. After meetings that went on for several days, Quiroga set off for the north and Rosas stayed on on an *estancia*, the Hacienda de Figueroa in San Andrés de Giles, where he wrote a long document dated 20 December 1834, which Quiroga received while he was in Santiago del Estero.

This is the famous letter from the Hacienda de Figueroa, one of the few documents in which Rosas explains his political thinking. Briefly, he claimed that the country was not yet ready to organise itself constitutionally under a Federal regime. It lacked the most basic requirements. It had just ended a civil war, the provinces were crushed and wounds still ran deep. If a congress were summoned, it would be filled with Unitarians, "lodge members and rogues" and would be an out-and-out failure. Besides, money was needed and there was none. Where would Congress meet? Not in Buenos Aires, as it would immediately awaken the provinces' distrust, as had always been the case. What type of constitution would they agree to write?

Rosas believed things would be straightened out over time. He thought that instead of imposing a top-down form of organisation on the country, matters should be solved by letting the provinces settle their affairs first, accustoming them to living in peace and creating their institutions. Only then would they be in a position to even begin considering a national constitution. In the meantime, they should try and live in harmony.

Although some staunch defenders of Quiroga the constitutionalist have held that this letter betrayed him, the *caudillo* was very likely to have agreed with Rosas. The letter is in the National Archives and has a bloodstain on it because it was in Quiroga's suit when he was assassinated at Barranca Yaco. His death meant the postponement, perhaps indefinitely, of the country's dream of a constitutional organisation. After 1835 Argentina lived through a period of confederation along the lines of Rosas' pragmatic thinking.

To sum up then, the Federal Pact, signed by Rosas as governor of Buenos Aires, Estanislao López of Santa Fe and Pedro Ferré of Corrientes, was a covenant whereby the three provinces promised firstly to defend one another in the event of foreign or domestic attacks; secondly, not to allow the dismembering of the country; and thirdly, to guarantee constitutional organisation when peace was restored. Facundo Quiroga agreed with the terms of this Pact and, although he never signed it, his opinion as the major political and military figure in the provinces still counted.

The alliance formed by the littoral provinces had the support of Quiroga, who fought against the Unitarian league. This was under the influence of General Paz, who had ousted several governors from power and replaced them with his own, mostly military, friends. Just a few months later, the Unitarian league was crushed following Paz's capture and Quiroga's campaigns, and their army disbanded. Indeed, after Rivadavia's disastrous government, the Unitarians had stopped believing so steadfastly in a centralist form of government. They realised that actions spoke louder than words and so began to regard centralism as a utopia. All they expected by then was some form of organisation for the country. Whatever the case may be, the Unitarians disappeared from the scene especially after Rosas' second government, and the political hegemony of the country represented by the various governors in the provinces became Federal.

CHAPTER V
TOWARDS A NATIONAL DESIGN

As part of the quest for a political formula that would give a reasonable degree of unity to the provinces, two agreements had been signed: the first was the federal Treaty of Pilar (1820), which aimed at a constitutional organisation that failed to materialise, and the second, the Federal Pact (1831) signed by Buenos Aires, Santa Fe and Corrientes and gradually adhered to by the other provinces. The Pact primarily committed signatories to summoning a congress once peace had been restored and adopting a federal system. Rosas' 1834 Letter from the Hacienda de Figueroa had a rather more theoretical approach and laid down his thinking on these matters. He believed the country was not yet ready for a constitution and that only time would tell.

ROSAS

Rosas' second government began early in 1835 and lasted for seventeen years until the Battle of Caseros in February 1852. I shall not go into the controversy over Rosas here in too much detail because, in my view, there has been so much polemic over him that it has drained the subject of any interest it might once have had.

Rosas had a rather personal idea of freedom: he considered that governments should be authoritarian and repressive, either implicitly or explicitly. He had no sense of tolerance or pluralism whatsoever towards his opponents; rather he believed in the need for a paternalistic authority directing every detail of life in the community. He was, besides, a staunch defender of Argentine sovereignty (referred to as 'independence' at the time) and courageously opposed the ambitions of the most powerful countries in the world, France and England.

Rosas is criticised or praised for widely differing personality traits, but there is no possible argument about him from the historiographical point of view. It is unlikely that any document shedding light on the most obscure aspects of Rosas' life as a man and a governor will ever be found. There certainly is a controversy about the values he represents that still stirs interest and emotions today. Those who value freedom as a fundamental part of a society will never like Rosas; those who believe in sovereignty as an integrating force in a nation will speak well of him, and so the controversy goes on and on.

Nevertheless, I shall review some features of Rosas' government. During his essentially conservative regime he made no changes and in a way even revived the character of the colonial system in that he did not allow any kind of debate that might lead to the fragmentation of society. He gave absolute importance to the concept of authority, and to some ideas he expounded during the Independence Day celebrations of 9 July 1836. This speech of his is not well-known. His contention was that the May Revolution had been staged to protect the king of Spain's lands and that nothing but the royalists' lack of understanding had led the *patriotas*, the advocates of Independence, to the inevitable declaration.

In many ways Rosas was still living in colonial times. As a reactionary, he gave religious matters and paternal authority great emphasis. No initiative whatsoever was taken to carry out public works: university life, for example, virtually came to a standstill from lack of funding, though a few departments did keep on lecturing thanks to students paying tutors out of their own pockets.

During his government, relations with the rest of the world were almost non-existent: foreigners were not chased away or discriminated against and there was a modest influx of immigrants, but no interest was shown in opening up to the rest of the world and new ideas from abroad. Quite the contrary, anything strange or foreign was looked on with suspicion especially by Rosas himself. Being a *criollo* and a nationalist, he was sentimentally attached to the land and its ways, no matter how primitive or barbaric these were.

His conservative attitude towards the country forged a sense of national unity which had not been able to mature until Rosas' day.

The long reign of the *Rosista* regime and its repetition of bureaucratic acts created a degree of unity the provinces had previously lacked because, although Rosas spoke of the Federation and raised the banner of federalism, he was in practice the head of an absolutely centralist regime and gradually created a de facto national government.

Shortly before his downfall, he had accrued a number of powers as governor of Buenos Aires that are practically the same as those the Constitution grants the President of the Republic today, and which in certain cases exceed the modern National Executive Power. Apart from handling foreign affairs, for instance, he kept a close eye on the border provinces to prevent the illegal trade in gold coins (nowadays known as a currency drain) and to block any incoming propaganda that might interfere with the federal system.

Rosas as governor of Buenos Aires was also the head of a sort of Ministry of the Economy, given that he collected duties from Customs in Buenos Aires, and in some cases, curiously enough, he sent subsidies to the provinces, who were badly in need of funds. Such was the case in Santiago del Estero, to which he sent money to rescue it from its state of economic stagnation. He had also set up something like a War Ministry since he controlled what we would nowadays call the National Army, which fought against Bolivia, part of the Banda Oriental and Brazil, and also later fought off England and France. Taking advantage of the fear Buenos Aires instilled, he intervened in any provinces that did not submit to his power by sending them simple letters or military expeditions, as in the case of the Northern Coalition.

Likewise, he was in charge of everything related to the clergy, such as the appointment of bishops or the passing of bulls and papal documents, and kept close watch on the religious orders and parish priests to make sure they adhered to the Federation's regime. Of course, he consistently censored the press and prevented any opposition periodicals, journals and books from abroad entering circulation.

But the fact that Rosas gathered to himself some of the powers the Constitution would later grant the national government created the conditions, once he had been defeated at the Battle of Caseros, for constitutional unity in Argentina.

CONSTITUTIONS

Another of Rosas' typically conservative stances was to pay no attention to the sign of his times. Given time, the rigidity that keeps things exactly as they were in the past can be useful to counteract dissent and chaos, but then in the face of new demands and needs, a highly conservative government will fail to pick up on them and absorb them, and that was exactly what happened with the *Rosista* regime.

In 1835 this may have been a necessary respite from the civil wars that had been tearing Argentine society apart. But afterwards there was reasonably sustained progress, and other intellectual and legal needs arose, such as a written constitution. Throughout the 1840s, popular revolutionary movements in Europe were demanding constitutional charters from or imposing them upon monarchs. The fashionable idea of the day was that the relationship between authority and subjects, between the various national authorities themselves, as well as rights of citizens should all be enshrined in writing in books or laws.

This need was also felt in the River Plate, but Rosas paid it no heed. When in May 1851 Justo José de Urquiza decided to stage a rebellion, all Rosas did to counter it was to publish his famous letter from the Hacienda de Figueroa written seventeen years earlier. For him no time had elapsed. He still believed that a long period in which things would sort themselves out on their own was necessary and that constitutional organisation would gradually emerge from below rather than being imposed from the above.

His government had become anachronistic. What had proved useful fifteen years earlier had now become meaningless. Nevertheless, Rosas was still the head of the most sizeable armies. Every governor followed him, as did the federal masses in Buenos Aires, apparently. Still, his government was crumbling from within and could no longer justify its actions.

In this sense, it is worthwhile pointing out that there were several Rosas according to which region his actions made themselves felt in. There was a Rosas for the city and for Buenos Aires Province, where he was most likely loved by the masses and respected by the middle class for being a guarantor of safety, imposing law and order and creating the conditions for the people to work and save. In 1847, for example, an Englishman by the name of William McCann travelled around Buenos Aires Province for a whole month and was lucky enough to always find lodgings with Englishmen, Scotsmen or Irishmen. Foreigners were respected and left to live their lives in peace, even during Rosas' steadfast resistance of France and England.

Moreover, in the Province of Buenos Aires a fairly stable peace had been reached with the native Indians, who staged no *malones* (raids) during Rosas' government. There was a system of 'incentives' whereby the government of the province sent them mares, tobacco and yerba mate so that they would stay on relatively friendly terms.

So much for the Rosas of Buenos Aires. When it came to the littoral provinces of Entre Ríos, Corrientes and Santa Fe, Rosas acted quite differently and was to trigger the series of events that led up to Urquiza's rebellion. This Rosas had a virtual monopoly on river navigation, having forbidden foreign ships to ply the rivers, and this stifled thriving economies such as in Entre Ríos, where salaries had been on a par with Buenos Aires and where there had been a great deal of trade with the Banda Oriental. There was not much sympathy for this Rosas. He was also the heartless subduer of the frequent rebellions in Corrientes.

Finally there was a Rosas for the other provinces, a figure both feared and hated: it was this Rosas who ordered the terrible campaigns led by the Uruguayan, Manuel Oribe, which left the cruel scars of their violence for a long time to come, and it was this Rosas who ordered the execution of José Cubas in Catamarca and Marco Avellaneda in Tucumán. The list of the provinces' grievances is a long one. They had been floundering in an economic mire while Buenos Aires had flourished. This state of affairs had to come to an end if the country wanted to organise itself: the inhabitants had to be granted their rights, and a definitive political system and fairer distribution of national revenues had to be enforced.

CASEROS

After the Battle of Caseros, Rosas vanished from the political scene and went into exile in England, and Urquiza took centre-stage. Caseros was not a battle between two opposing sides in which one side (Rosas') was defeated; it was more the result of the Federal party's own infighting. After Caseros the old *caudillo* was left aside and the new one stepped forward.

A series of anti-Rosas factions had become Urquiza's allies. These included the old Unitarians such as Sarmiento or Mitre, or rather those who claimed to be Unitarians but were actually liberals living in exile. The Brazilians too, whom Rosas had declared war on a year before, strengthened Urquiza's expeditionary force, helped him with river navigation and ultimately made his victory at Caseros possible.

Urquiza's government of Buenos Aires Province was moderate. The new centre of political power mainly consisted of liberals and old Unitarians. *Porteños'* pride had been wounded because Rosas had not been overthrown by Buenos Aires but by an expedition from the provinces, very similar to Ramírez and López's in 1820, though this time more spectacular.

After Caseros, Rosas resigned as governor and the Legislature was dissolved. Under Urquiza's new regime, elections were called, which the *Porteñistas* won. A new legislature was elected and Vicente López y Planes was voted in as caretaker governor. Then Urquiza, with a commitment to the country to draw up a constitution, summoned all the provincial governors to San Nicolás de los Arroyos and the San Nicolás Agreement was signed. Along with the Treaty of Pilar and the Federal Pact, this agreement forms part of the set of pre-existing agreements referred to in the Preamble of the Constitution.

The San Nicolás Agreement was reached by governors from Rosas' times, who were assimilated to the political order founded by Urquiza. Rather than confronting them, Urquiza wanted to use them as political instruments in this new institutional stage. The San Nicolás Agreement was important in several ways: firstly, it was a waystage on the road to a General Constituent Congress, which was to be made up of two representatives from every province, and would meet in Santa Fe. Being allotted the same number of representatives as Jujuy or La Rioja rubbed Buenos Aires up the wrong way.

Secondly, it paved the way for a future constitution by abolishing internal duties, declaring people's freedom to migrate and abolishing domestic taxes on merchandise crossing Argentine territory, as well as free navigation of rivers. As well as practically creating a common market within Argentine territory, the Customs in Buenos Aires Province was to be nationalised, which meant that revenues from customs which had up until then been allocated to the province itself would be distributed throughout the country.

Thirdly, the intention behind the agreement was to create a provisional government called the *Directorio*, or Directoire. Urquiza was appointed Director and given certain powers including commanding the country's militias and looking after the national treasury, which mainly meant handling Buenos Aires' customs revenues.

The signing of the San Nicolás Agreement was quite a bold act on the governors' part in that none of them were invested with the power to make such a commitment. Still, it demonstrated their determination to organise the country despite its conflicting interests. The *Porteños* in particular had arguments against it, which even had some basis in law, and these were expounded by Bartolomé Mitre to the Legislature in Buenos Aires.

According to Mitre the governor of Buenos Aires, in the first place, had no powers in San Nicolás to avail himself of goods that belonged to the province such as its natural resources or troops. Secondly, reading between the lines, Mitre claimed that Buenos Aires had no interest whatsoever in nationalising its assets, such as its Customs or the city itself, which might be made capital of the Federation.

Mitre's statement made the Buenos Aires Legislature reject the Agreement, though it was signed by all the other provinces. Feeling deprived of his authority, Vicente López y Planes resigned. Urquiza staged a coup and took over as governor of Buenos Aires. However, there was strong opposition from within the province, and finally in 1852 the *Porteños* regained control over the city by staging another revolution. Urquiza tried to lay siege to the city but failed and had to retire.

A few months later, representatives from the provinces met in Santa Fe (though none came from Buenos Aires), approved the 1853 Constitution and elected Justo José de Urquiza president, a highly precarious situation that was to last ten years. On one side, there was the Argentine Confederation, an entity of thirteen provinces that aspired to embodying the Nation as a whole. It had a National Constitution sanctioned by the congressmen in Santa Fe, a Congress and an Executive Power whose headquarters were in Paraná. Ambassadors and consuls went there to discharge their duties but, finding the city rather dull, soon left for Buenos Aires.

On the other hand, there was a State of Buenos Aires, whose position was ambiguous: it did not declare its sovereignty or its independence; it did not call itself a free State, neither did it belong to the Confederation. For practical purposes, it was taken to be an autonomous state that recognised itself as part of the Argentine Republic.

SEGREGATION

Buenos Aires' secession, which could have thwarted the movement towards national unity indefinitely, set one national body in Paraná against another entity in Buenos Aires. Each competed against the other, sometimes even militarily. The reader may be wondering what obstacles were really preventing them from uniting. Primarily, this boiled down to an economic and socio-political chasm between progressive Buenos Aires and the rest of the country, just as there had been in Rosas' day.

Buenos Aires already had gas-lighting on its streets by 1857, as well as a railway that stretched to San José de Flores and a Customs House built to meet the needs of growing trade. Entre Ríos, second only to Buenos Aires in terms of progress, did not even come close, never mind Santiago del Estero, Córdoba, Tucumán and the others. These lay in the hands of *caudillos* from Rosas' day and the ruling class was not as enlightened as it was in Buenos Aires. Their universities, legislature and press were not so deeply rooted or substantial as the

Porteños'. The differences were so great that it was difficult to find an answer to the question of national unity.

The Argentine Confederation hardly had any permanent source of income, whereas Buenos Aires had the Customs House to meet its needs. Revenue was also used to bribe the head of the Confederation's fleet laying siege to Buenos Aires, or to raise armed National Guards to fight Urquiza's cavalry from Entre Ríos, who may have been a colourfully dressed company but were useless for offensive purposes. There was also a more radical group in the Confederation that wanted to force Buenos Aires to join it, while in Buenos Aires there were those who even wanted to declare it an independent republic. In the end, both sides turned their back on these extremes and chose the reasonable path.

The reason behind segregation's demise was that both sides came to understand that Buenos Aires could never become an independent country and the provinces could not do without Buenos Aires. This idea dates back to the former Viceroyalty: Buenos Aires and the provinces may have been very different, but they were also complementary and any differences between them had to be thrashed out.

The patriotism of some of their leaders also contributed to national unity. It is evident that Urquiza wanted to bring the country together once and for all and, although he was from the provinces, he understood that any such organisation was impossible without Buenos Aires. This in some way goes to explain his subsequent attitude towards the Battle of Pavón.

And finally, history itself was a factor: Argentines had been seeking a way to live in harmony for fifty years ever since the 1810 Revolution. They had plenty in common: historical events, national heroes, the memory of the great epic of Independence, and the fact that some of the leading lights of those events were still alive made segregation a great sin.

All told, these factors led people to believe that, regardless of conflicts and confrontation, it was possible to find a lasting solution. This was finally achieved, but only after two great battles, one of which was the Battle of Cepeda in 1850 when the Confederation defeated Buenos Aires. Here again Urquiza proved his moderation because, instead of entering the city, he set up camp in San José de Flores and simply requested that governor Valentín Alsina, who was an extremely vehement *Porteñista*, be removed and replaced by someone it would be possible to talk with.

This led to the historic Pact of San José de Flores whereby Buenos Aires committed itself to becoming part of the Confederation, which in turn would recognise any reforms in the Constitution that the provinces might wish to introduce. The issue of a capital city, however, turned out to be very controversial indeed. The first draft of the 1853 Constitution stated that the Capital of the Argentine Nation would be the City of Buenos Aires, which the *Porteños* found intolerable because it entailed handing the city over to national authorities they were unlikely to be able to control.

Therefore, one minor amendment was that the capital would be a city named by special act passed by Congress, and before which the Legislature of whichever province having to hand it over would meet for a special session. So, if Buenos Aires was declared Capital by the National Congress, the *Porteños* could decide whether or not to pass a law that gave the city to the Nation at large.

The Pact of San José de Flores, which was a sequel to the Treaty of Pilar, the Federal Pact and the Agreement of San Nicolás, was the last step towards organisation on a national scale, the last covenant standing between Buenos Aires and the Confederation. But once the province had gone through the National Constitution, suggested amendments and sent their representatives to a special session of Congress, events led to another falling out between the Confederation and Buenos Aires.

Troops from either side lined up against each other near the site of the Battle of Cepeda and in 1861 the Battle of Pavón broke out. From a military point of view neither side was the victor since, although Urquiza's cavalry won, the *Porteño* infantry led by Mitre managed to advance as far as Rosario and Urquiza retreated to his quiet haven in Entre Ríos.

When the Confederation's government realised that Urquiza was not going to offer any more assistance, it adjourned and was dissolved.

Mitre, in turn, sent troops to the provinces to win over those who were against him, and managed to get several governments to invest him with the powers to handle foreign and domestic affairs that Urquiza had had after Caseros (in spite of Mitre's criticisms at the time).

Elections were held in 1862 and in the same year Bartolomé Mitre was sworn in as President of the Nation on October 12. Buenos Aires had already been reincorporated into the nation and had become its provisional capital after a law was passed by the Legislature whereby instead of handing the city over, the national government was invited in as Buenos Aires' guest, a subtle legal strategy to avoid actually naming it as the country's capital.

A NATIONAL GOVERNMENT

This long and inevitably confusing story brings us to a national government. This government had to quell rebellions in the provinces by means of brute force, above all those instigated by Chacho Peñaloza, who defended the defeated Confederation with the scarce means he had at his disposal and for his troubles was later murdered. But for the first time since 1822 there was an official, truly national government.

This solution only lasted a couple of decades, but it was appropriate at the time. The provinces had a Constitution and the Buenos Aires Customs House gradually learnt to allocate its revenue in favour of national needs. There were constitutional guarantees and independence of the powers-that-be as well as some kind of an ideological framework.

This framework had been proposed by Juan Bautista Alberdi in his book *Bases y puntos de partida para la organización de la República Argentina* (Foundations and Starting Points for the Organisation of the Argentine Republic). When Urquiza gathered the Congress that approved the 1853 Constitution in Santa Fe, its members had begun to look for models to follow. Although they had a fair idea of what they were looking for, they lacked any knowledge of the practical side. It was then that Urquiza came across this book. Alberdi was an Argentine lawyer who had left Buenos Aires for Valparaíso in Chile some twenty years earlier after a disagreement with Rosas. He had an outstanding professional career.

In this work Alberdi put forward a draft Constitution and laid the theoretical foundations of the new country that was beginning to take shape. He put Rosas' dictatorship and the long civil wars firmly in Argentina's past and prepared for the country to take on a different role both at home and abroad.

I shall summarise the contents of Alberdi's book in my own words: "Let us write a Constitution in which every kind of guarantee is given to the people who wish to come here to work, set up industries, teach, educate themselves and spread their ideas. However, let us not be so liberal in politics. There is no electorate or citizenry. Argentine has no citizens yet. Native Argentines have not yet acquired good habits of work or respect for authority. They have nothing that makes a normal government possible.

What is to be done then? Foster immigration. Let plenty of foreigners, especially Anglo-Saxons, come and mix with our native population. Then with the children and grandchildren of these immigrants a new type of Argentine will be born: that will be the moment to grant political rights. In the meantime, let us, the most capable, the best, handle things by obtaining foreign investment, building railways, rationally exploiting the Pampas. Thus we shall, little by little, be creating the conditions for the birth of republican forms with republican meanings. Meanwhile, let us stick to the mere form of a republic."

The truth is that this was a very down-to-earth way of putting things, but it was the kind of thinking that emerged in Mitre's times and later prevailed during Roca's government after 1880. In other words Alberdi meant to say: "Let's build a thriving country, let us try to establish relations with the rest of the world, open our frontiers to immigrants, capital and ideas but, for the time being, let's forget about political rights, because the conditions for a perfect republic are not yet ripe. This is not the United States or Europe".

But in the meantime, as society grows richer, prospers, and acquires the physical and cultural assets of civilisation, as well as peace and order, we shall be creating the conditions for better politics when the right time comes. For now, the people will not be entitled to vote or if they do, elections will be rigged so that the natural leading class may continue to rule." Again, this was very pragmatic thinking and it pervaded Argentine life and thought until 1912, when the Sáenz Peña Law granted suffrage to all male citizens over eighteen years old. Some people at least now had the right to vote.

CHAPTER VI
THE SHAPING OF INSTITUTIONS

The period between 1860 and 1880 laid the foundations for Argentina's final constitutional organisation. Like perhaps no other in our history, these crucial twenty years reveal that communities are not created in fits and starts and that absolute ruptures with the past are very rare. Continuities in life, work, customs, attitudes, beliefs or even prejudices are always there to be seen. With time they gradually fade into other continuities but are not usually abruptly interrupted. If they ever fade away completely, they do so only to become the fountain-head for new forms in the future.

This is just what happened in the years we shall be looking at in this chapter. The conflicts and civil wars of the years before 1860 were appalling, yet although between 1860 and 1870 fearsome clashes also took place, they tended on the whole to become less violent. Society was evolving and new institutions were being set up which tempered the brutality of previous years.

Argentina was still very sparsely populated but was constantly evolving and, in general, improving. It was receiving a steady trickle of immigration and colonists. Railways were being built and political infighting channelled into something that resembled ideology.

THE WORLD AT LARGE

These two vital decades cannot be understood without some reference to the international context and the momentous changes, both qualitative and quantitative, taking place in the outside world.

The 1850s witnessed the second to last great war of the nineteenth century in Europe. The Crimean War between Russia on one side and England, France, Turkey and Sardinia on the other, was a testing ground for new military techniques and strategies. In the United States in the early 1860s, the Civil War broke out. This led to the triumph of the industrialised North against the romantic, feudal, slave-owning South of the cotton plantations. In 1870 the Franco-Prussian War broke out, ending in the defeat of France, the fall of Louis-Napoleon's empire and the creation of the German empire.

From that moment on there was peace in Europe and the world at large (with the exception of a few colonial wars of course). European societies were expanding and developing thanks to a handful of inventions which affected people's quality of life. These inventions also reached our shores: gas-lighting spread from the streets to people's houses thus allowing people to read more and promoting literacy among the population. New high-temperature annealing processes in steel manufacture led to innovations in the construction industry. It was a time of great medical advances: previously unknown micro-organisms were discovered. Railways lurched across the world.

These years between 1870 and 1890 also brought great advances in the quality of life even for Europe's working classes, who benefited from cheap, fast transatlantic travel which let them emigrate to other continents. Indeed, the industrial workers of England, Germany and France were living far better than their parents or grandparents had, and required a variety of products that our country and others in America supplied them with. In other words, the international scene was marked by peace, the availability of capital for foreign investment, and scientific and technological advances.

POLITICAL MECHANISMS IN ARGENTINA

Meanwhile in Argentina, between 1860 and 1880 three presidencies followed one another. These were, so to speak the Republic's 'founding' presidencies: Bartolomé Mitre's from 1862 to 1868, (although he had effectively been running the country from 1860 after his victory over Urquiza in the Battle of Pavón), Domingo Sarmiento's from 1868 to 1874 and Nicolás Avellaneda's from 1874 to 1880, all consolidated the republican system.

This sequence of dates is a clear indication of constitutional continuity; in other words, the age of the *caudillos*, of governments toppled by uprisings, of lengthy periods of dictatorship was over. These three sets of dates mark three six-year periods, and although elections were not always cleanly fought, the fact that these presidents were all able to see out the terms granted to them by the Constitution was a great advance.

This was not a sudden change of direction but rather a reaffirmation of what had already been taking shape. Argentina sought to avoid being ruled arbitrarily by a handful of politicians holding all the public authority, or by *caudillos* representing provincial authority, by looking instead to presidents appointed for a given legal period.

How were politics conducted over these years? How were leaders elected? In what way did public opinion make itself felt? Broadly speaking it could be said that after the Battle of Pavón Mitre found himself in control of the situation and built a power base in the provinces and Buenos Aires that would lead to him being made president in 1862. He was relying on a party known as the Liberal Party, because it recognised that he had embraced the standard of liberalism.

Liberalism meant little in the provinces but a good deal in Buenos Aires: well-founded institutions, free journalism, parliamentarianism, the opening up of trade, freedom to manage profitable industries. However, the Liberal Party inherited major problems such as deciding on the new nation's capital (a problem Urquiza had had to deal with back in 1853): *Porteños* were reluctant to make their city not just the capital of the Province of Buenos Aires but of the Nation.

As I have said, to solve this problem a bit of legal skulduggery was indulged in: the Province of Buenos Aires became host to the Nation's government and invited it to settle there for a while. Through what was called the Law of Compromise, Buenos Aires became a provisional capital. The National Government set up its headquarters on the site of the Viejo Fuerte (Old Fort) where the Casa Rosada now stands, while the Province of Buenos Aires maintained its jurisdiction over the city. Both the Nation's and the Province's legislative bodies used to meet at the site of today's National Academy of History, which is where the old Legislature of Buenos Aires and the National Congress used to stand.

When the Law of Compromise was resolved, the Liberal Party was divided. The more strongly pro-Buenos Aires, *Porteñista* side, with Adolfo Alsina at the helm, raised the banner of autonomy, and designated itself the Autonomist Party. On the opposing side were the liberal *Mitristas*, or Mitre supporters. Apart from these factions, there was the old Federal Party that had backed Urquiza. When all was said and done, this was a party made up of the dregs of the power structure that had kept Rosas in office for so many years and still prevailed in the provinces. These were not political parties in the modern sense of the term. They had no constitutional bodies or party machinery proselytising on a permanent basis. Federalism as led by Urquiza, *Mitrismo* and Autonomism were simply trends that leading politicians used to sign up for. Within this framework they would spin their alliances, confrontations and rifts.

On the eve of elections quaint institutions called "clubs" would suddenly spring up. These were, so to speak, the forerunners of 'committees'. The Liberty Club and the Buenos Aires Club called on the population to meet in squares or theatres and an executive committee chaired the session. Lists of candidates would then be voted on and statements and manifestos passed. Then the club would be dissolved until the next time. This was a primitive form of democracy and lent itself to all sorts of Athenian trickery.

In his *History of Sarmiento*, the modernist poet and novelist, Leopoldo Lugones, tells us that the Liberty Club had to choose between Sarmiento or Alsina. So one scorching summer afternoon the president of the club, a Sarmiento supporter, asked Sarmiento's followers to vote by standing in the shade and Alsina's by standing in the sun. Of course, everyone chose the shade and the Liberty Club accordingly picked Sarmiento.

Elections were as fraudulent as ever and always left a toll of dead and wounded. Without a civic electoral register, permanent authorities and identity documents, anyone could vote four or five times. Authorities could turn people away from the polling tables because they were not from the local parish or, conversely, people could turn up to vote in five or six different parishes. Nevertheless, democratic republican practices were beginning to unfold which in Rosas' day had been brought to a standstill and after Urquiza's victory at Caseros had been accompanied by extreme violence. There was now at least some respect for the results whatever the implications.

Although this political system did not consist of constitutional parties, it did prefigure such a system. It was crowned by two practices which became very widespread in their day. There was journalism, or *diarismo* as it was known at the time from the large number of newspapers or *diarios* disseminating opinion and framing debates for the public at large. Both paper and labour were extremely cheap and as a result every fairly important political leader had a newspaper at their disposal. *La Nación*, Argentina's most prestigious daily, started out life as Mitre's own personal newspaper. Moreover, gas-lighting was making reading easier and written media served as organs for disseminating opinion, selecting candidates and debating issues that affected the community, such as the Indian question, where the port of Buenos Aires or various railway lines should be built and under what conditions... Political debate was being taken to the populous.

The other democratic practice was parliamentarianism or the custom of exercising one's right to an opinion in the Legislature and National Congress where there were fixed rules in debates and discussions were supposed to be orderly and reasonable. Here, oratory was practised as a kind of sport and, at a time when there were no mass media other than newspapers, it played a vital role. No political leader could afford not to be a great orator. Some, like Adolfo Alsina, José Manuel Estrada or later Leandro Alem were, according to tradition, mesmerising and drew large crowds. This parliamentary pastime was however a step forward in a period with no public participation or representation on legislative bodies.

These three presidencies then strengthened constitutional continuity and accustomed the country to obeying the law. It was not that infractions did not exist, but it is curious how much guilt was expressed whenever things got out of hand. On the occasion of scandalous electoral frauds, or unjustified interventions in the provinces, or excessive interference from the ruling party, this guilt normally took the form of attempts to cover up or justify the transgression.

Obviously this was a step in the right direction. An unprovoked slap in the face is one thing: for example, Lavalle's report to the delegated government in Buenos Aires when, with quite indiscriminate brutality, he told them: "Gentlemen, I hereby inform you that Colonel Dorrego has been shot on my orders". However, the kind of journalistic and legislative debate created in a situation like, say, Urquiza's assassination by the revolutionary from Entre Ríos, Ricardo López Jordán, is quite another thing. We may or may not, as the case may be, find the series of justifications that were given acceptable, but they do nevertheless indicate some regard for the law. Institutions such as the National Supreme Court and federal judges in the provinces, who to some extent are the custodians of the Constitution, both belong to this period.

IMMIGRATION

At the same time as these political practices were getting under way, other developments were contributing to Argentina's progress, to an improved quality of life for its inhabitants and the rational exploitation of its natural and human resources. One of these was immigration.

Juan Bautista Alberdi, Domingo F. Sarmiento and all the men who after Caseros had been preparing to lead the country, had great faith in the arrival of thousands of Europeans who would populate the Pampas and teach its inhabitants habits of work, thrift and respect for authority as yet unknown in Argentina and whose dearth was, in these men's opinion, preventing the people from governing themselves.

Alberdi's answer was to create a society that offered its citizens every guarantee to prosper, work, educate themselves, travel about and own property free from abuses, but one in which they would not yet be able to vote and elect representatives. Alberdi proposed that the republican structure should be kept but that a small group of enlightened men should in practice manage the country, amongst whom he naturally included himself.

Immigration, it was presumed, would given time produce the mould for a new kind of Argentine: an industrious man who understood about machines and lacked the wild and wasteful calling of the countryman. This was the moment when Martín Fierro, the hero of José Hernández's epic poem of 1872, made his appearance as the archetypal *gaucho* now in his fading years, but also when Estanislao del Campo ridiculed *gauchos* in his *Fausto* of 1866. Immigration, it was hoped, would raise the ethnic level and mentality of Argentine *criollos*.

However the immigrants who subsequently arrived were not exactly the ones that Alberdi or Sarmiento had in mind. Where possible, they wanted Anglo-Saxons with the same mentality they had seen in the United States: self-sufficient, politically self-determining smallholders who did not rely on handouts from the government. Between 1860 and 1880 immigrants, though not of the type just described, began to arrive in moderate but significant enough numbers for the government to draft an immigration policy and in some cases grant them property in colonies that were being set up in Entre Ríos, Santa Fe and to a lesser extent Buenos Aires.

Around this time too, the first railway lines were laid. These, in Alberdi's opinion, were the best instrument of communication and integration for a country where enormous distances meant long delays. Straight after Caseros, both the men from Buenos Aires and Paraná strove to entice capitalists and technicians over to lay railway tracks.

The conditions of the early contracts were leonine to say the least. The *Central Argentino* line running from Rosario to Córdoba stipulated a gift for investors of a league of land on each side of the tracks. The *Central Argentino* would turf out the settlers along its route and then set up subsidiary companies to sell the plots wholesale to various people. Nowadays we would look on the richest land in the country being given away like that with near horror, but this was a regular occurrence in high-risk countries like Argentina, and was even done in the United States and India, both with similar distances to cover.

By 1870 the railway stretched from Rosario to Córdoba and in the Province of Buenos Aires there was also the *Oeste* or Western line reaching the south of the province as far as Chivilcoy and Chascomús. The rail network so typical of Argentina was begun. It would later all converge on the port in Buenos Aires. Meanwhile, a handful of investors, almost all of them British, were beginning to show interest in building railways over here.

Another feature of these two decades was sheep farming, a way of exploiting the countryside that may seem anachronistic to us now but was in those days a handy means of pushing back the frontiers of usable land, as far as Indian territory at least. Buenos Aires Province was essentially a sheep-producing province. Sheep had an advantage over cattle: their birth cycle was fast and they produced a large number of offspring. They could be exploited both for wool and meat, which was treated in the *saladeros,* or salting plants, and exported. Wool was a staple product especially at a time when standards of living in Europe were rising and ordinary people were looking for higher quality coats.

Among immigrant sheep-farmers were many Irishmen who had been driven over in the 1840s and early 1850s by the Great Famine that ruined several potato harvests. Many emigrated to the United States and Argentina, where they were welcomed by characters such as Father Fahy, who would point them in the right direction and take them to places where he could find them work with one boss or another and possibly an Irish wife into the bargain.

A farmer who arrived without a red cent was supposed in two years to be able to put together a good-sized flock of two or three thousand sheep. It was sheep then that pushed back the frontier of agricultural Buenos Aires and not cattle. Nowadays sheep are looked on as almost predatory animals but in those days their grazing habits cleared the tough grasses and made way for more digestible ones that cows could eat.

Immigration and sheep-farming in the province of Buenos Aires and the new colonies in Entre Ríos, Santa Fe and the east of Córdoba thus began to define Argentina's economy. It did not yet amount to much in terms of world production or consumption but it was searching for its place via a rudimentary agriculture and the exploitation of its few known workable natural resources.

DIFFICULTIES

The same period had its negative side, too. Firstly, an absurd war with Paraguay broke out in 1865. It was a product of the extremely delicate balance of power in the River Plate region as well as of the Paraguayan dictator Francisco Solano López's megalomania, Brazil's expansionist zeal, Uruguay's weakness and the alliances of Mitre and his friends, the Liberal Uruguayan *colorados*. This explosive mixture led to a war that lasted five years and brought no benefit whatsoever to Argentina despite its eventual victory. It was a war that brought appalling plagues to Buenos Aires and the whole Littoral area. Its only positive outcome was the forging of a national army.

Until then there had been no national armed force but only provincial militias or national guards (which despite their name were provincial too). The War of the Triple Alliance as it has come to be known, pushed many young patriots in Buenos Aires to enlist in the Army. The provinces were obliged to send recruits who were generally drafted against their will. The camps of the War of the Triple Alliance sparked off many a young officer's career and the National Army's function in the future was clarified, namely, to support the State.

Apart from the war, three rebellions broke out in Entre Ríos during this period. In 1870 Ricardo López Jordán spearheaded a revolution which culminated in the assassination of Urquiza in his San José Palace. From then on Sarmiento either had to live with the situation or send the army into Entre Ríos. He decided on the latter course of action but, as López Jordán had the backing of the population, the intervention led to a protracted war that came to an end in mid-1871 only to be repeated twice more against López Jordán's various other revolts. Although the insurrection of 1870 was not against the State, Sarmiento could not afford to turn a blind eye. Quelling it ate up a good deal of arms, money and time, and left a blemish on years which in other ways are clearly ones of progress.

The problem of revolutions beset virtually every new president's assumption of office. It is well-know how Mitre came to power: backed by the national regiments' bayonets in their efforts to eliminate Federalism and set up governments that would later support his candidacy for president. Sarmiento's assumption of power passed peacefully but when he left the presidency, the confrontations between Adolfo Alsina and Mitre or Nicolás Avellaneda and Mitre turned bitter. The struggles resulted in an insurrection led by Mitre, which lasted several months and was finally quashed by General Rivas in Buenos Aires Province and General Roca in Santa Rosa, Mendoza. The unrest of 1874 was to break out again in 1880 when Avellaneda left power.

Nevertheless, the meaning of these constant revolutions, provincial mutinies and disturbances was different in that they were no longer utterly arbitrary but demonstrated a certain respect for the law. The pretext was generally that fraud or some undue interference from the national powers-that-be had been committed and in some ways this signified the more widespread respectability of the law.

Another issue was the Indians. In Rosas' day, peace had been kept through a rather ponderous system of bribes and donations to the Indian chiefs. After Caseros though, the Indians not only organised raids and entered Christian towns but in some cases took part in the civil wars as well. They would side with Urquiza or Mitre and became a political force not to be ignored. Calfucurá, a highly intelligent chief, managed to bring together a loose confederation of tribes in the Pampas and thus boosted his offensive potential.

In those years of relative prosperity, sheep-raising, *estancias* and *saladeros*, the Indians from the south of Mendoza, north of San Luis, south of Córdoba and the west and south of Buenos Aires province posed a constant threat to Christian populations and operations. Nevertheless, these days of settlement were prosperous and the Indian problem was soon solved with the *Conquista del Desierto*, the Conquest of the Desert. But at precisely this moment, 1879, two developments appeared in the wings that would later have an enormous impact on life in Argentina.

THE WHEAT AND THE COLD

And then there was wheat. The first exports were made in 1878. They were only small but until that year Argentina had generally had to import it from the United States. From 1878 onwards there was a small surplus to sell abroad. But in the space of only thirty years this was to become the most important of Argentine exports.

In 1879 a piece of technology appeared that was to be of enormous significance. In that year a ship that could reproduce cold conditions artificially, Le Frigorifique, transported several tons of frozen lamb to Europe. Part of its cargo was lost when a section of the refrigeration machinery broke down but the rest reached France in good condition and was consumed.

Preservation, the old bugbear of the ranchers that had kept them awake at night since colonial times, was in the process of being solved. In the days of the *vaquerías* carcasses were left in the countryside for mice or dogs. Then came the era of the *saladeros* in which the meat that had previously been wasted was macerated, dried, salted and sent in barrels to market. Even though these markets had a low turnover, they nevertheless made products from the *saladeros* (some of which employed several thousand people) an exportable commodity.

But the real problem was how to preserve meat in such a way that its quality did not offend the European palate. In around 1870, the Rural Society in Buenos Aires Province offered a substantial cash prize for the person who invented a technique to preserve meat in this condition. It was a Frenchman, Charles Tellier, who discovered how to produce cold artificially and what in 1879 had been just an experiment later came to have immense significance for the Argentine economy.

Meanwhile, Mitre was endeavouring to get Buenos Aires and the provinces to live together in peace, and Sarmiento was trying to set up schools across the country and thereby slowly change the customs and mentality of Argentine society through education and colonisation. Avellaneda strove to overcome the dreadful economic crisis that befell the country in 1874-75. This forced the government to cut spending significantly but did not prevent it paying back the debts it had run up. Avellaneda also implemented a kind of experimental protectionism by imposing high customs tariffs. Quite unintentionally, these new rates favoured a handful of developing national industries, especially those like the leather and wool industries that relied on raw materials produced at home.

In the meantime, political struggles were raging. Members of the Liberal Party, now divided between Liberals and Autonomists, were fighting each other for power. In 1877 they reached a conciliation: Adolfo Alsina would succeed Avellaneda when the latter had seen out his term in 1880. Although this conciliation of the two sides did not make everyone happy and elements from both *Mitrismo* and *Alsinismo* rebelled, it was nevertheless a civilised political pact that allowed one to view the future with some optimism. Alsina's death in 1877 brought the conciliation policy down in flames and a new star appeared in the firmament. This was General Julio A. Roca, who had successfully waged the Desert Campaign against the Indians and was beginning to find support in the old guard of the *Alsinistas*. The *Mitristas,* on the other hand, stood against him. Roca also found support in old-style Federalism from the provinces (now dispersed after Urquiza's death) and from mid-1879, only just back from the Desert Campaign, prepared himself to fight for the presidency of Argentina. Julio Roca, sponsored by his brother-in-law, Juárez Celman the governor of Córdoba, came up against Carlos Tejedor, the governor of Buenos Aires, who was backed by *Mitrista* and *Alsinista* elements. Instead of being a simple struggle between two presidential candidates, this clash unleashed a complex struggle with the Nation at large on one side and Buenos Aires Province on the other. The Nation stood behind Roca's candidacy despite President Avellaneda's reservations, while the city of Buenos Aires and the countryside around it stood behind Tejedor.

The showdown between the two sides led to armed confrontation (though this can hardly be termed a revolution since it was the national government itself that began the hostilities) between Buenos Aires and the Nation in the months of June and July of 1880. This resulted in more than a thousand dead, almost all of them *Porteños*. There was a virtual siege of Buenos Aires until its provincial government surrendered to the national government. After moving its seat to Belgrano town, the latter expelled the *diputados*, or deputies (the Argentine equivalent of MPs in the UK or representatives in the US), who had sided with Buenos Aires and filled their posts with ones chosen *ad hoc*.

Finally, seizing on the moment of Buenos Aires' defeat, occupation and disarmament, Roca decided to put a daring end to the city's pretensions to becoming the Nation's capital. He forced through a law that proclaimed Buenos Aires the capital of the Republic. In other words, what the 1853 Constitution had originally stated was finally made reality in the law of 1880, which moreover was passed by special act from the province which ceded the common land of the city of Buenos Aires for use as the capital of the Nation and ended the old balancing act between Buenos Aires and the provinces, a leftover from the last years of the Viceroyalty. From then on, the city lay in the hands of the National Executive Power, which had direct jurisdiction over it. As a result, Buenos Aires Province had to choose another capital city, the city of La Plata further down the coast.

A YEAR OF FOUNDATIONS

So 1880 was a year of foundations for various reasons. Firstly, it marked the end of the Conquest of the Desert. The Indians were expelled from their land and 15,000 square leagues lay at the feet of progress. Secondly, two significant developments that went unnoticed at the time became a fact of life: the exportation of small quantities of wheat and the successful preservation of meat in cold storage. Thirdly, and most importantly, when Buenos Aires became the Nation's capital with Roca's presidency, the true foundations of the National State were laid. Argentina's institutional wrangling was over.

Until then there had been virtually no National State, since it had always been a lodger in, a guest of Buenos Aires. In the turbulent days before the 1880 Revolution, faced with complaints from provincial deputies asking him for guarantees, President Avellaneda would point to the policeman standing at the corner of his house and say "What guarantees am I going to give you when I don't even have any power over that policeman out there?"

From 1880 onwards, the State acquired an importance and strength that it had previously not possessed, due to problems arising from its relationship with the Provincial Government, often the stronger of the two. The Bank of the Province of Buenos Aires, for example, was much more stable than the National Bank. After 1880 the State had a permanent seat and sufficient resources to set up structures that would be spread nationwide: national schools, federal courts, army garrisons, sanitation works, the *Banco Hipotecario* (Mortgage Bank), the *Banco de la Nación*; in short, what Roca called the duties and functions of the State.

So 1880 was a very important year all round and the figure that embodied the process was General Roca, a native of Tucumán and barely thirty seven when he became president. With some extraordinarily lucky breaks he had climbed the political ladder until at thirty-one he had become General of the Nation and managed to unite *Porteños* and provincials alike in promoting him as a figure of national unity.

In conclusion, it could be said that during the years between 1860 and 1880 the outline of a nation was being filled in, a blueprint for *fin-de-siècle* Argentina. Although many positive and negative elements from the past still survived, the world scenario, changes in society and the will of a handful of leaders converged in the construction of a country which was quite consciously carving out an identity for itself and defining its role on the world stage. This was the Argentina of the years between 1880, the first year of Roca's presidency, and the Sáenz Peña Law of 1912.

CHAPTER VII THE SHAPING OF MODERN ARGENTINA

The years between 1880 and 1910 (or rather the milestone 1912 Sáenz Peña Law) have come to be known as the Conservative Order or Conservative Regime. Yet here the adjective 'conservative' is not being used properly. The prime movers of political, economic, social and cultural activity over this period were not actually conservatives. Their intentions were not so much to 'conserve' as to modify. The epithet owes its existence to the fact that the major political forces of these years began to call themselves "conservative" after 1912, and it was these forces that laid the foundations for the conservative parties that came after them.

THE *BELLE ÉPOQUE*

Over these three decades the rest of the world was also living through a unique period. The *belle époque* was characterised by peace in Europe (the last war it had seen being the Franco-Prussian War of 1870) and by 1880 France, who had blundered into a republican system almost completely by chance, had reinforced the strength of its economy and the solidity of its political institutions and once again become the figurehead of Europe. The German empire on the other hand, which had been founded on France's defeat, tended towards a highly centralised imperial regime. Bismark had already disappeared but his theories on how to shore up the empire were still very much alive. Kaiser Wilhelm II's warlike urges soon turned his country into something that put the fear of God into the rest of Europe.

Great Britain had also strengthened its power base and after the Boer War the world map was predominantly pink due to its extensive overseas possessions. It was without doubt the outstanding world power and possessed an enormous fleet, a massive trading base, vast industrial wealth and remarkable institutional stability.

The United States was beginning to flex its muscles, quite spectacularly so in its 1898 war against Spain in which the Spanish fleet was sunk off Cuba by an overwhelmingly superior American fleet.

On the one hand, this meant that the United States began to implement an imperialist policy leading to its virtual occupation of Cuba, the Philippines and Puerto Rico, and to imperiously encroach on pan-American affairs. On the other hand, the Spanish, who for the first time in the century were enjoying a stable (party) political system, suffered the defeat in Cuba as failure on a national scale. Its consequences were above all literary and cultural with the generation of 98 undertaking a searching self-criticism sparked off by events in Cuba.

Apart from the Cuban and Boer wars the world lived in almost complete peace and stability during this period: capital was plentiful and European emigration to the Americas remained steady or even increased. There was at the turn of the century a certain optimism in the air.

Unlimited universal progress, the elimination of nationalist movements, the lessening importance of religious ideologies, the standardisation of political and economic regimes across the globe (where currencies were in practice interchangeable and the international business establishment suffered no obstruction or interference whatsoever) were all cause for reasonable optimism. It is there in the books, novels, theatre and cinema of the period, and it was widely believed that absolute world stability had been achieved. Although this state of affairs was to collapse in 1914 with the advent of the First World War, these were essentially the features that characterised the Conservative Order in Argentina.

A NATION IN EMBRYO

These three decades were witness to the birth of modern Argentina. If an average twenty-year-old Argentinian had taken a look at his country around 1880, he would have seen a country with fairly promising prospects and valuable natural resources but lacking a capital city and a State apparatus, a country in which a third of the territory was occupied by Indians and which had no currency of its own nor importance on world markets; in other words, a country that might at some stage function well but that for the time being still had a long way to go.

Thirty years later, the same Argentinian would have seen the most advanced country in South America with a natural and profitable place on world circuits of investment, production and consumption; a country that could boast the longest railway network in Latin America and one of the longest in the world. Argentina had an admirable education system and differed from other American nations in possessing a sizeable middle class and previously unknown political and institutional stability. Our Argentinian, who at twenty had seen a country pursuing maturity, could by the Centenary celebrations of 1910 be justly proud of this genuine success story.

1880 was the first year of Julio Roca's first presidency. Buenos Aires had already been made capital of the Republic by the Legislature of Buenos Aires Province and the National Congress. The State had been structured in such a way that, in the president's own words, it would have to be above any disturbance or revolution. In other words, it had to possess the necessary authority to act as the real arbiter of any conflicting interests within the Nation itself.

Between 1880 and the 1912 Sáenz Peña Law we can speak of three fairly distinct political periods beginning in 1880 with Roca's presidency when the National Autonomist Party was in power. This was an amalgam of the old *Alsinista* party (or at least a small part of it) and provincial groups who had supported Roca and become far and away the major party of government.

The Autonomist Party's ascendancy continued into the presidency of Roca's brother-in-law, Miguel Juárez Celman (1886-1890), who intensified the ruling party's clannishness by proclaiming that the leader of the National Executive Power would also be the ruling party's sole leader. There were virtually no other parties to speak of, although 'parties' is almost an abuse of the word when defining what amounted to little more than cliques in which the president of the Republic, legislators and provincial governors together made up a close-knit web of political interests.

In 1890 the system suffered a critical setback with the *Revolución del Parque* (Park Revolution) and the emergence of an opposition party, the *Unión Cívica* (Civic Union), which a year later became the *Unión Cívica Radical* (Radical Civic Union). Juárez Celman subsequently bowed out and Roca returned to the stage to try and make the now precarious regime he himself had set up years earlier a viable proposition.

Roca realised that the exclusivist way of governing that had been the hallmark of both his own and Juárez Celman's presidency had come to an end, and that in future the State's authority would have to be based on a convergence of political forces. This was what drove him to seek an agreement with the *Mitristas*, who had been almost completely excluded from official life since 1880, when they had been defeated in Carlos Tejedor's Autonomist uprising against Avellaneda.

After 1891 then *Mitrismo* began to side with a regime from which it did not feel too estranged despite certain differences. The agreement weathered the political storms of 1891, when *Radicalismo* in the form of Bernardo de Irigoyen launched itself into an aggressive electoral campaign. It also withstood the dreadful year of '93 and a spate of Radical revolutions throughout the country. The agreement survived and not only propped up Carlos Pellegrini's presidency (1890-1892) but also helped him pull the country out of economic crisis. It put Luis Sáenz Peña in power, though he resigned in 1896 and was replaced by his vice-president José Evaristo Uriburu. 1898 marked Roca's second presidency, where he remained until 1904 when Manuel Quintana took charge. Quintana died two years later leaving his vice-president José Figueroa Alcorta in charge. In 1910 it was Roque Sáenz Peña's turn to be replaced after his death by his vice-president, Victorino de la Plaza, who in 1916 passed the torch on to Hipólito Yrigoyen, the first president elected by universal vote according to the new electoral regulations.

Summarising the Conservative Regime, we can identify a first period stretching from 1880 to 1890, marked by the exclusivism of the National Autonomist Party; a second beginning in 1891 and characterised by the lasting agreement with *Mitrismo*, the mainstay of the system throughout the 1893 and 1905 revolutions; a third period beginning with Quintana's presidency, in which General Roca's political legacy was replaced by forces that in 1912 would pass the Electoral Law. We shall now go on to look at a few ideas that characterise the period.

IDEOLOGY

In the first place, Juan Bautista Alberdi's ideology was put to practical effect over this period to create a civilian society offering its citizens a whole range of guarantees and the right to gather wealth and educate their children, but not as yet granting them full political rights for fear they would not exercise these sensibly. There was an enduring spirit of reconciliation between parties, who, despite particular differences, agreed on the broad principles of the proposed society. Whether they were supporters of Roca, Mitre, Pellegrini, Sáenz Peña, Udaondo, or the Modernists, they all agreed to defer any electoral reform that allowed the vote to be handed unconditionally to the masses. They shared a policy of opening Argentina's borders to the outside world to allow an influx of men, ideas, merchandise, capital, even fashions.

Such was the ideology common to the "generation of the '80s", though this was not so much a generation as two or three hundred loosely-grouped personalities scattered around the country. They had for the most part been educated at the same schools and universities, spoke the same language, shared the same ideology and customs. They knew each other well and some were even good friends. They were capable of waging fierce contests for power but ultimately held the same opinions about the country's destiny and its relationship with the outside world.

Argentina thus made inroads into world markets through intelligent, rational exploitation of the land using the technology of the day to achieve maximum profitability. This phenomena has been much studied but the collective effort involved still never fails to amaze: the fact that, without planning or flow charts or seminars or anything of the sort, Argentina did exactly the right thing at the right time; in other words, exploit the land, its one great resource, by introducing a handful of technologies which were by then relatively cheap and accessible, and whose effectiveness was well proven.

The first of these was wire fencing, widespread use of which only came about in the 1880s. Wire fencing meant that landowners' property materialised before their very eyes and put paid to the vagueness of colonial days according to which so-and-so's property stretched from this ombú tree to that bank of the stream. The wire perimeter fence marked out precisely where the limits of one's property were and, more importantly, made possible the division of the countryside into lots for pasture. Wire fences and cattle gates permitted a clear division between agriculture and cattle farming and prevented sown fields being trampled by cattle. Thanks to the new system moreover the handling of *rodeos*, or cattle round-ups, was rationalised: calves could now be separated from their mothers who could in turn be sent to the alfalfa fields to be fattened up.

Another extremely important piece of technology was the Australian wind-pump which meant there was water wherever it was needed. These used wind-power to force water from underground into Australian-made tanks and it meant that ranch-owners no longer needed to look for lakes or pools, rivers or streams for their animals to drink from. The area of land that could be exploited was thus greatly increased.

The first steam seed drills and combine harvesters also began to make an appearance, making farm work far lighter and allowing farm-hands and the ox-ploughs to be replaced by heavy machinery that did a more efficient job.

The other key piece of technology, again not of Argentine invention but which changed the face of the Argentinian countryside, was cold storage. Since the days of the *vaquerías*, ranchers in Buenos Aires had been racking their brains to find a way of preserving their meat so that they could offer a product that was a cut above the salted meat only slaves could stomach.

Once the first refrigerated ship had successfully transported its first cargo to Europe in 1879, refrigerators began to be installed and the switch was made from frozen lamb to beef to cater to the European palate. There was an increasing demand for fattier, tastier meat from animals that matured more quickly and this led to the beginnings of cross-breeding; up to then cattle had tended to be of the scrawny, horned varieties with long legs suitable for roaming over long distances.

The face of the Argentine countryside changed as did the *estancias*, which became large trading centres. The old *criollo*-style ranch-houses were replaced by French-style houses or Norman castles. Production was so profitable that in little less than thirty years Argentina became the primary exporter of cereals in the world and the second largest exporter of frozen meat after the United States.

DEBTS

To erect these fences and wind-pumps, to cross-breed cattle and sow crops, capital investment was needed and generally speaking landowners were prepared to run up debts to do it and this was one of the causes of the crisis of 1890. Nevertheless, capitalising on the countryside was an intelligent strategy. Owners would lease out sizeable strips of their estates mainly to immigrant farmers, or *chacareros*, who paid in kind or cash according to the contracts. This brought about what James Scobie, an American researcher, has called the "Pampas Revolution": the transformation of land as yet rationally unexploited into an abundant source of oil-bearing crops and cereals.

The transformation of countryside and economy was one of the essential features of this thirty-year period. Through its exports (which balanced out the 1890 economic and financial crisis) a previously peripheral country found its place on the world stage, where ever since it has had not only a commercial but a social presence in the form of travellers, the rich *estancieros* settling in Paris to live, be cured, die or simply amuse themselves.

Very soon Argentina was being talked about as an El Dorado, an image that was corroborated by almost all the travellers visiting the country most of whom left in amazement at the transformations taking place. Argentina was aglow with optimism, a mood not too different from that in the outside world. However, Argentina had material proof for its confidence. New cities such as La Plata and many others sprang up; railways were laid in the middle of nowhere; provinces such as Mendoza and Tucumán, where the wine and sugar industries were protected, fairly brimmed with prosperity.

These factors along with its rapidly burgeoning middle class placed Argentina streets apart from other Latin American countries. Here there was an affluent, oligarchic, generally land-owning class and an enormous swathe of the population living more or less as they had done in colonial times, while Argentina had a population of white immigrants whose children enjoyed compulsory education that developed almost hand in hand with immigration and pacification policies.

IMMIGRATION, EDUCATION, PEACE

The Conservative Regime's policy then can be said to have depended on three rudimentary principles. The first of these, immigration, was one of the most constant and faithfully maintained of Alberdi's ideas. He had had in mind Anglo-Saxon-based immigration that would gradually change Argentines' ethnic make-up, teach them work habits, respect for money, authority and so on. Although the immigrants who disembarked were not Anglo-Saxon (when he saw Poles, Jews, Arabs and Syrians arriving Sarmiento blustered: "These aren't the immigrants we were looking for"), they nevertheless contributed cheap labour and introduced new diversity into a population that was dwarfed by the expanse of the country.

In this sense, the immigration policy carried forward by the governments of the Conservative Regime was expansive and in no way discriminatory. Nobody was turned away. Even Roca in his first presidency appointed a special immigration agent to try and divert the stream of Russian Jews fleeing to the United States in the wake of the pogroms. Towards the end of the century a few Jewish colonies began to spring up in Buenos Aires and, although at times voices were raised in protest against some types of immigration, no restrictive laws were ever passed.

The second of the three State principles was education. In this respect the Conservative Regime was truer to Sarmiento's thinking than Alberdi's. Sarmiento's insistence on the need to educate the sovereign power was gradually brought into force after 1882 when the National Board of Education was set up and primary schools began to proliferate all over the country. These were the institutions that were to provide the national schools already created by Mitre and Argentina's two traditional universities, Córdoba and Buenos Aires, with their students.

The primary school system especially was an admirable enterprise. We should bear in mind that Article V of the Constitution had laid down the development of primary school education as part and parcel of the State's respect for the autonomy of the provinces. And given that some provinces could not sustain the necessary level of primary education (wealth had not increased evenly across the board after 1880), the 1905 Láinez Law established the Nation's obligation to help them.

The care the Regime's governors' put into primary education does them credit because immigration plus popular education inevitably meant that ten or twenty years later there would be a new generation, the children of immigrants wanting to take their place on the political stage and govern the country. The men in the Regime knew that this would in the long or short term mean their eventual displacement yet they chose education and passed Law 1,420 according to which primary education became obligatory, free and secular (in that citizens were guaranteed that their children would not have to make confession).

Immigration and education were two of the mainstays of modern Argentina; the third was peace, the deliberate decision not to get embroiled in any conflicts with its neighbours.

What today goes without saying was in those days a critical decision as there were outstanding border disputes to be settled. Though Argentina and Brazil were on fairly good terms, the same could not be said for Chile or Bolivia, and resolving border problems, with Chile especially, in order to avoid a potentially ruinous arms race was a constant headache not only for Roca and Pellegrini but also for Mitre.

In 1902, after various crises and treaties, Argentina and Chile bowed to the British king Edward VII's arbitration and through the celebrated *Pactos de Mayo* (May Pacts) an abiding status quo was reached. There were however moments of tension with Brazil: Estanislao Zeballos' policy under Figueroa Alcorta could have taken matters right to the brink, but this was eventually defused by the manoeuvring of men like Roca, who urged that Argentina should maintain a pacifist stance not only on principle but also because of a basic belief in the long-term returns that peace would bring.

THE STATE

Quite apart from policies of immigration, education, peace and open borders; a system that avoided conflict by way of pacts and a general feeling of optimism, Argentina had a State that worked. Until 1880, as I have said, no such State existed; only a government based in Buenos Aires that lived at the expense of others and controlled a national armed force created during the Paraguayan War. It was, however, powerless to fend off attacks, either armed or verbal, from provincial governments or political forces, as was the case for example in 1874.

After 1880 the National State not only had a capital but was also bolstered by the creation of important bodies such as the National Board of Education or the *Banco Hipotecario Nacional*, and ministries such as Public Works or Public Instruction. Moreover, it had an army which with the introduction of national service was now legally recognised; so much so that in the civilian-military disturbances of 1890, 1893 and 1905, the army remained loyal to the government and its institutions, despite the participation of a good many soldiers on an individual basis.

It is going rather too far to say the Conservative Regime was liberal. Much of its thinking was liberal, as was its belief in free speech and a free press. In one way, even its stimulation of the economy by opening up the borders was liberal. But these men were still very clearly aware that the State had to be strong and authoritarian in order to act as permanent arbitrator in the community's various competing interests; that it had duties and functions it could not shirk.

When Juárez Celman, dogged by the economic crisis of 1889-90, put 24,000 leagues of fiscal lands up for auction in Europe, which were never sold; when he leased out the national water and sewage company, the *Obras Sanitarias,* in Buenos Aires and sold off some of the nationally-owned railways, Roca, the architect of the Conservative Order, complained bitterly to a friend of his. If it was true that governments are bad administrators, he said, we would have to auction off the barrack houses, post and telegraph offices, the inland revenue and customs, and everything that went to make up "the duties and functions of the State". In other words these so-called promoters of liberal thought knew that a country in embryo such as Argentina needed a firm hand from the State, not in order to interfere with private initiative but rather to mark out its inevitable limits and promote the development of areas that the private sector would not have anything to do with.

QUESTION MARKS

With immigration, with the creation of an industrial infrastructure, the newly established proletariat began to voice social grievances and the claims of anarchist or socialist leaders permeated the least advantaged classes. Especially after 1904 and 1905 the system, which in many respects had been so progressive, began to become more repressive. A Law of Residency was passed and some members of the Regime were worried that upheavals were on the way that would lead to their eventual overthrow or downfall.

In fact they had no serious reason for alarm. There were strikes and unrest but at no time between 1900 and 1910 could repression have been justified. Rather this revealed a fear that had not been present in the founders of the Conservative Order: neither Roca or Pellegrini, or Mitre himself, nor Sáenz Peña senior or junior ever dropped their optimistic tone where the fate of the country and the character of its people were concerned. But the last avatars of the Regime, men such as Marcelino Ugarte and others, were terror-stricken about what these rabble-rousing anarchists and socialists might do. The repressive laws and police involvement marked a turning point in once generous policy-making.

In any case by around 1910 or 1912 the Conservative experiment had achieved what it had set out to. The country proposed by Alberdi, which in 1880 was still on the road to development, was now, in 1910 at the very forefront of Latin American life. It was the most ingenious transplant of European civilisation that had ever been seen.

There was, however, one aspect of politics that remained to be reformed, one that provoked not only the criticism of impartial bystanders but also constant protest from the Radicals: the politics of the pact, the agreement, the alliance. Though these had their use in avoiding conflicts and confrontations, they nevertheless made for an utterly illusory and at the same time deeply immoral electoral system. The power-sharing that had characterised the regime for years was undoubtedly a weak spot in a republic which in other ways was a success story. It corrupted public life, discouraged the best men and imbued parliamentary proceedings with an aura of falsehood.

This was when Roque Sáenz Peña, constrained by a series of factors we shall be looking at further on, proposed a bill for the laws that now bear his name and which brought about a drastic change in the country's policies. The Sáenz Peña Law replaced the slippery, fraudulent, violent electoral regime of previous years with a system in which citizens could vote freely, where runners-up in elections would also have a political say through the *lista incompleta* (incomplete list) whereby minority candidates could also govern alongside the eventual victors.

The Sáenz Peña law was passed to clean up an untenable situation. The men who had built the republic, Mitre and Alberdi, were dead and gone but their political heirs had a perfect right to believe that the electorate would go along with the ratification of their legitimacy because of their previous successes. In just thirty years they had turned a splintered, peripheral, anarchic country into a leading force in Latin America. And yet the electorate turned its back on the original masterminds of modern Argentina and embraced an unknown quantity: a new force with no coherent programme of its own and a faceless leader.

The thirty years between 1880 and 1910 were crucial ones in the making of modern Argentina. In a way we are still today the heirs to this age. The great public buildings and parks to be found in every Argentinian city date from this time. The strengthening of the country's basic institutions, from primary education to universities and the Armed Forces are the result of a regime that, though it committed many political sins, did however have a keen sense of Argentina's future role in the world at large.

THE PRICE OF PROGRESS

The prosperity of this period depended to a large extent on production of the so-called humid Pampas: first on cereals, then on oil-yielding crops and above all on meat. As a result the most privileged region was one that took in much of Buenos Aires Province, the south of Santa Fe, the south of Córdoba and part of San Luis. Also privileged were the wine and sugar-producing areas.

However certain regions of the country whose production was of little interest were excluded from this prosperity and the infrastructure that went with it (such as the railway network converging on the port in Buenos Aires). The mining and craft industries of the northern and north-eastern provinces in these years suffered from neglect and subsequent backwardness. As the provinces of the littoral grew at a rate of knots, there were others, Catamarca for example, that had flourished under the Confederation but were to lose out under the Regime.

Demographically speaking, increasing poverty was reflected in censuses and, politically, in parliamentary representation, which depended on each province's population and was adjusted after each census. With the passing of time it became clear that the provinces of the north and north-east had less parliamentary representation compared with the littoral provinces. This had serious repercussions: when certain public works were voted on there was a bias towards the littoral provinces according to the wealth they created and the other provinces, the original founders, remained bogged down in underdevelopment.

Social growth was also uneven. Many people made fortunes and a class of thriftless snobs began to appear, while other sectors of society were suffering the consequences of a fiercely competitive process in which there were no social safety nets. The starving starved and anyone thrown out of a job ended up on the streets with no compensation whatsoever, and that was all there was to it.

There was no welfare state to speak of. What did exist however was a guarantee from a well-oiled State machine, namely, that the Argentine peso would keep its value, and this in turn meant an opportunity to save. A peso once deposited would be worth exactly the same five, ten, twenty years later. This made it possible for anybody with a bit of luck and the good sense to save to make purchases in instalments, acquire land, build themselves a house; to feather their nests for retirement.

These were times of uneven but prodigious growth, which contained within itself the instruments for self-correction, such as that which made the transference of power from an elitist to a popular system possible. The history of the shaping of modern Argentina is one of admirable progress; progress that did not come about by accident but was sensibly promoted by a core of clear-thinking leaders working in conditions that would never be so favourable again.

CHAPTER VIII
RADICAL DEMOCRACY

The further we go in our account, the wider the range of subjects becomes and the harder it gets to summarise an increasingly complex social situation. Therefore, I will from now on be looking at events from a political angle, although also I shall of necessity be alluding to the conspicuous economic, social and cultural features in the coming periods.

The period I will be discussing in this chapter begins in 1912 with a great step towards democracy, the Sáenz Peña Law, and ends in 1930 with the first founderings of democracy. The year 1930 marks the beginning of a phase in which the armed forces came to play an active role in Argentina's political affairs. Nevertheless, between 1912 and 1930 there was perfect constitutional continuity and the interaction of political parties acquired a reasonable degree of pluralism and tolerance. This was the shining exemplar of Argentinian parliamentary history, and it was marked by the prominence of the Unión Cívica Radical, *the Radical Civic Union.*

THE *UCR*

So far any detailed discussion of the Radical Civic Union (*UCR*) has deliberately been avoided but now is the time to deal with this, the leading light of civic-mindedness in Argentina; a party that had pushed for the Sáenz Peña Law guaranteeing compulsory universal male suffrage with the 'incomplete list' system. Radicalism was not only the grand designer and executor of this law but also its beneficiary as of the first elections, notably in 1916 when Hipólito Yrigoyen was elected President of the Nation.

Radicalism has undergone several changes in its political platform over the years; only natural for a party that is now more than a century old. Even by 1916 it was a very different party from the one founded by Leandro N. Alem. In September 1889 a political group called the Civic Union was created out of the politically disparate *Mitristas*, old guard Autonomists and Republicanists, Catholics disaffected at Roca and Juárez Celman's secular laws, and even young men with no previous political experience. In July 1890, on a platform aimed at fighting corruption, election rigging and the kind of single-party policy embodied by Juárez Celman, the Civic Union staged a revolution with the backing of certain sections of the military: this has come to be known as the *Revolución del Parque*. Though the uprising was quashed, it brought about Juárez Celman's resignation and his replacement by Carlos Pellegrini as well as a new political set-up symbolised by the presence within the walls of the *Parque de Artillería* (the Artillery Park in Buenos Aires where the Courts now stand) of men such as Leandro N. Alem, Bernardo de Irigoyen, Juan B. Justo –founder of the Socialist Party– and Lisandro de la Torre, founder of the Progressive Democracy movement. This event was quite simply a watershed in Argentinian political history.

In January 1891 the Civic Union announced Bartolomé Mitre as their presidential candidate and Bernardo de Irigoyen as his running mate, a prize-winning ticket. Mitre was the most prestigious name in the country and Irigoyen was not far behind. Another of this combination's assets was that they symbolised the union of two great historical trends in Argentinian politics: Mitre was a staunch *anti-Rosista* and an out-and-out liberal, while the Autonomist Irigoyen had served in the Rosas regime as a young man. By running together these two great personalities stood the best chance of overthrowing the regime built up by Roca and epitomised by Juárez Celman.

However Roca, who was Interior Minister, either out of policy or patriotism, came up with the idea of reaching an overall agreement that would do away with elections and avoid the confrontation he was predicting. Therefore, he asked Mitre to be the candidate not only for the Civic Union but for his own *Roquismo*. Mitre accepted straightaway. He was probably convinced that this was solution before Roca's offer because, although he was in Europe when the

Revolution took place, he had received news from his many friends about the political solution Roca was hatching.

The important thing is that Mitre agreed to be the candidate for virtually all the political forces in the country by giving up his right to choose the other half of the ticket, in other words he agreed to the *Roquistas* putting their own candidate forward to replace Bernardo de Irigoyen. This was a bolt from the blue for the rank and file of the Union, who accused Mitre of striking the same personalist attitudes as he had criticised in his *Roquista* and *Juarista* opponents.

THE REVOLUTION

After much bitter argument, the Civic Union split into two factions: the *Mitristas*, who in various guises lasted until 1910 or 1912, and the Radicals under Leandro N. Alem. (In his speeches Alem was fond of stating that he was 'radically' against this or that agreement, and the name stuck.)

The 1891 Convention of the brand new Radical Civic Union announced Bernardo de Irigoyen as its presidential candidate and conducted the very first Argentinian election campaign. Alem travelled around most of the republic, only occasionally accompanied by Irigoyen, who was a little old to be rushing about so much. He stirred up much enthusiasm in the provinces, which led the party to set up branches almost everywhere, not just in its Buenos Aires homelands.

The *UCR* was unique in several respects. Firstly, it was a party that flew the flag of revolution: not revolution as a future alternative to a poorly functioning electoral system, but revolution as a permanent goal, a drastic way of shaking up the established order.

Radicalism staged a revolution in 1893 when Alem himself organised an uprising in Rosario followed by insurrections in Buenos Aires (led by Alem's nephew, Hipólito Yrigoyen), Tucumán, San Luis and two in Santa Fe. 1893 was a hard year for the government of Luis Sáenz Peña, who had accepted the presidency after Mitre had pulled out of the race on realising that he was not cutting the figure of national unity he had wished for.

Especially after Alem's death, Yrigoyen kept the torch of revolution burning and this policy paid dividends in 1905 in a huge, revolutionary uprising of civilian and military forces that initially met with great success. They managed to take key cities such as Rosario, Bahía Blanca, Mendoza and Córdoba, (though not Buenos Aires) but were defeated after three days. Despite defeat, Yrigoyen continued to wield his rhetoric of revolution and Radical activists spoke of the coming revolution as something inevitable. There are records of speeches by Radical leaders dating back to as early as 1907 and 1908 that end by urging the audience to join in the next Radical revolution and promising that this time it would not fail.

Secondly, particularly under Yrigoyen, Radicalism also selflessly chose to tread two very rough roads. The first of these was intransigence. By 'intransigence' Radicals meant dogmatically rejecting any kind of pact, conciliation or alliance with other parties: they flatly refused to enter into the kinds of agreements that are so common in power politics in civilised nations.

The reason why Radicalism took this stance was that it appreciated that the movement was more akin to a civic crusade than a political party. It rescued, with historic ramifications, the best of Argentina's past and represented the good citizen's struggle against the evil Regime. Consequently, Radicals did not see themselves as part of the political system and shunned any kind of alliance.

The second road chosen by Yrigoyen was abstention. This meant not participating in elections and generally refusing to play the regime's game. The Radicals were right to think that conditions for free voting had not yet been established. They refused point blank to participate in rigged elections and regarded them as a farce typical of the shameful regime they were denouncing.

These three features (revolution, intransigence and abstention) gave Radicalism the quality of an 'antisystem'. It was not a political party integrated into the legality of the system but one that called the existing official structures into question and posed a real threat with its constant calls for revolution, abstention from elections and refusal to enter into alliances.

Under normal circumstances, this stand would have been regarded as nothing short of suicidal: a party that had no apparent aspiration to take power, acknowledged no alliances and insisted on the revolutionary cause even after the Army clearly did not agree with it (although the 1905 revolution had been backed by many young officers, it did not have the support of the forces as a whole).

Yrigoyen had to be a stern leader in order to hold his party together under these conditions. Just think what a rare sight it was towards 1910 for a political party to have a nation-wide organisation with local headquarters in all the big city boroughs, its own newspapers and a coordinated system of associations, committees and conventions, yet not to take part in elections. Radical militants found it strange and unsatisfactory from a political standpoint, and Yrigoyen on several occasions had to use all his authority to withstand rebellions within the party, which usually came from upper class members desperate to reap the usual honours of republican life.

AN UNDEFINED AGENDA

If power was not the Radicals' aim, the reader may be entitled to wonder what their objective really was. The short answer is that it was a mystery: in the early stages of Alem's leadership, this boiled down to a call for public morality, transparency in elections and the continued enforcement of the federal system. But these are simply prerequisites for good government. No party would normally call for "administrative morality" since it is already supposed to exist; by the same token, it should not be necessary to call for "electoral freedom". Alem's objective was therefore not particularly clear, which explains Carlos Pellegrini's claim that Radicalism was not so much a party as a feeling.

The same is true of Yrigoyen's leadership: he systematically refused to lay down any kind of platform for his party, to the extent that in 1908 he broke off political relations with the provincial Radical leader, Dr. Pedro Molina, who had been calling for a commitment from the Radicals to protect the provinces. In a famous, controversial series of letters between the two men, Yrigoyen claimed that Radicalism's civic crusade was so important that asking him to stoop to trivia such as protectionism or free trade insulted the nobility of his mission. A few years later in 1916, when the *UCR* Convention appointed Yrigoyen as candidate, his friends torpedoed a proposal for a highly detailed election manifesto. As a result, the party's rhetoric advocated nothing more than abiding by the Constitution (which was no platform to speak of either, since any party wanting to be part of the legal system has to abide by it).

The fact that Radicalism kept calling for revolution and fostering conspiracy is one of the mysteries of Argentinian political history. But curiously enough, these very attributes gave it great strength and a clear identity when compared to the personality cults of *Roquismo*, *Pellegrinismo*, *Modernismo* and *Mitrismo*. The panoply of party names disguised their power-sharing practices as there were no laws governing political parties and names could constantly be changed.

Within this political kaleidoscope, Radicalism was conspicuous for its ethical conduct and this won over public opinion especially among the young. Its members were from all walks of life: Patrician families, urban workers, country labourers, *estancia*-owners; a striking sociological amalgam that cut across class barriers. When Ricardo Rojas joined the party in 1932 he stated, "I went over to Radicalism and was welcomed by the grandchildren of national heroes and the sons of immigrants."

Yrigoyen may well have refused to draft a proper manifesto for any future Radical government precisely because of its heterogeneous make-up. The pretext of abiding by the Constitution was a clever way of avoiding any clear-cut commitment to promises which might later draw criticism from various sectors of society.

THE FIRST ELECTIONS

Between 1906 and 1910, after Roca's years of domination, a man with no political power whatsoever, José Figueroa Alcorta, presided over the country. Carlos Pellegrini, Bartolomé Mitre, Bernardo de Irigoyen were all dead by this time. Roque Sáenz Peña had returned from Europe with the idea of perfecting Argentinian democracy, an important issue among the intellectual and ruling classes, and was appointed president in 1910. He remained in office until 1914, by which time Argentina was doing fairly well for itself: in just thirty years the various governments had succeeded in importing European civilisation to a lawless, badly-off country with no currency or capital city of its own, a third of which was occupied by native Indians. By 1910 however, it had become the paragon of European civilisation in South America: Argentina's level of education was extraordinary; it had a thriving middle class unlike other parts of the continent, stable national institutions and a distinguished ruling class.

Nevertheless, election rigging was still the name of the game and Sáenz Peña felt it was time to introduce some changes. He called on Yrigoyen to choose two or three Radical ministers for his cabinet but the *caudillo* refused, arguing that all his party wanted was to be able to vote. Yrigoyen's answer was a mark of his political genius, for if his party had joined the cabinet it would have been trapped. Thus Radicalism remained aloof from the negotiations and continued to plough its single-minded furrow of revolution, intransigence, and abstention.

Sáenz Peña sponsored a regular civic register overseen by the courts and the army to ensure that people could vote freely; that they had an enclosed voting space to stop any outside interference; that independent overseers would be present; and, last but not least, that there were 'incomplete lists' to promote the formation of two major parties by offering a reward to both the winner and runner-up (though this was hardly an incentive for the party that came third.)

And so, pressure to abandon their policy of abstaining from elections began to mount within the party. Yrigoyen refused, arguing that he did not trust the government to keep its promises, but he could not withstand the pressure that came from Santa Fe in the first ever elections, which were held in March 1912. One would have expected the Argentinian electorate to back the men who had turned the country around over the last thirty years but their priorities turned out to be different: instead, they preferred to back Yrigoyen's twenty-year-long ethical stand, his refusal to participate in election rigging or under-the-counter distribution of government posts, and his demands for the kind of electoral law the country now enjoyed.

The Radicals won Santa Fe and a week later Buenos Aires, where the Socialists were runners-up. Over the next few years, with Sáenz Peña's death in 1914 and Victorino de la Plaza as president, the Radicals' majority was consolidated but Radical and Socialist deputies began to question previous governments. Hipólito Yrigoyen's election by popular vote in 1916 marks a new era: the ascendancy of Radicalism.

However, what the Sáenz Peña Law had envisaged, viz the formation of two major parties, never came about. The reader might justly expect Radicalism to have governed with a Conservative opposition which, by mustering its pre-1916 forces, would bring to bear its long experience of government. Instead, the Conservatives chose to infiltrate certain newspapers, the Senate, the financial sectors and diplomacy, and failed to offer a democratic counterpoint to Radical rule. In some cases Yrigoyen took control of some provincial Conservative administrations arguing that they had been elected fraudulently and Radicalism inexorably came to reign supreme.

GOVERNMENT ACTION

Yrigoyen also had to deal with the wider problems of his day. The Great War for example: was Argentina to remain neutral? Were relations to be broken off and sides taken? On the home front, should the university students be supported or suppressed? What should be done about the railway and building workers' strikes that were affecting the economy: put pressure on employers or support them?

Yrigoyen, who came to office during the First World War, had to maintain Argentina's neutrality, though this was sometimes hard to do. Imports were thin on the ground while Great Britain, Germany and France were at war. To complicate matters further, factories were closing down for lack of raw materials. Since certain goods could no longer be imported, they began to be manufactured at home, thus opening up the prospect of a national industrial base to accompany the growing agrarian sector such as the meat and cereals needed by the warring countries.

Yrigoyen's government did, however, uphold both its neutral stance and the prevailing economic structure. It put no obstacles in the way of the land-owning oligarchy and saw to the demands of university students. The Radicals under Yrigoyen carried out a revolutionary egalitarian agenda quietly and with no fuss. Countless second generation immigrants benefited from a statutory public education which enabled them to go to school and university or allowed them access to the civil service without discrimination, both in an electoral and administrative capacity. The days of nepotism and snobbery in public office were numbered.

Apart from this, the Radical political ascendancy left its mark on the social, economic and cultural fields. Culturally speaking, there was a return to more national motifs in music, poetry and painting: the architect Martín Noel for example, who began to value the beauty of the chapels in the northeast and colonial architecture in general. There was a renaissance of folk music and, in the book world, Ricardo Rojas wrote his *History of Argentinian Literature*. But although the Radicals patronised an intriguing movement that tried to distance itself from motifs from abroad, they never really changed the foundations of Argentinian life.

RADICAL ASCENDANCY

In the meantime, their achievements permitted moderate prosperity, an improved standard of living for the working classes and consolidation of the standing of the middle class, who felt flattered that their children could hold public posts. The thrall Radicalism held over life in Argentina reached the point that, by 1922, it had hardly any opposition other than the Socialist Party in Buenos Aires and minor factions in the provinces.

But there is a law in political science whereby, when a party holds a country in unanimous thrall, opposition comes from the very core of the party. When affairs are conducted at national level in such a way that a wide variety of opinion cannot be expressed, then the struggle is played out within the ruling party. This is precisely what happened during the 1920s, when in 1924 a split occurred between Antipersonalists and *Yrigoyenistas*.

The Antipersonalists were against Yrigoyen's personalistic *caudillo* swagger, while the *Yrigoyenistas* thought that their antagonists were nothing but bigoted right-wingers in disguise and that they were the only ones who really understood the popular, revolutionary and Americanist nature of Radicalism. These struggles gave birth to a fascinating Radical intellectual movement, which through books, pamphlets, articles and the 1928 election campaign brought coherence to what, during Yrigoyen's government, had merely been a series of decisions on miscellaneous subjects.

Everything Yrigoyen had done on the international stage, or in the area of social, economic and educational policies was given a coherent thread by young *Yrigoyenista* intellectuals. This brought Radicalism into line with other Latin American parties such as the *APRA* in Perú and the *PRI* in Mexico, both of which had a firm foothold in the populace and tended towards moderate statism and anti-imperialism, in other words, a centre-left party.

In 1928, when Alvear's six-year term was up, there was infighting between the *Yrigoyenistas* and Antipersonalists, the latter supported by the conservatives and a breakaway faction of Socialists called the *PSI* Independent Socialist Party. These struggles ended with a landslide victory for Yrigoyen known as 'The Plebiscite' because the Radical *caudillo* managed to get twice as many votes as all the other parties put together. Nevertheless, this victory later backfired on Yrigoyen when the Radicals began to wallow in their achievements and turn a blind eye to what was really happening.

The popular support, which Radicalism believed would go on forever, rapidly dwindled within two years for several reasons: the ageing Yrigoyen made several mistakes, while adamantly anti-Radical, anti-democratic action from various tendencies who thought Radicalism would be hard to displace in future elections sought the expediency of conspiracy. It should be remembered at this point that Italian fascism had been very successful in the twenties as an alternative to capitalism and communism; Primo de Rivera's mild and bloodless dictatorship had restored law and order in Spain and Germany was in the first stages of Nazism.

Faced with the sorry spectacle of the smug Radicals rallying around Yrigoyen and trusting to grass roots support, many parties began demanding a hierarchical government depending neither on the masses nor elections, but which better represented the interests of society. This brings us to the eve of the 1930 revolution, a decisive moment in Argentinian history that marks the beginning of the armed forces' encroachment on the political arena and a general distrust of democracy. Imperfect as it was, democracy had acquired civilised, pluralistic habits of tolerance which from now on were on the wane.

I wish to point out at this stage that from the very first chapter, the subjects we have discussed are all in a way related to the present: when we looked at the foundation of Buenos Aires, we portrayed the rivalry aroused between Buenos Aires as an inland gateway and the land-bound provinces; when we analysed the creation of the Viceroyalty, the clash between Buenos Aires and the provinces was as intense as ever; and when we discussed the *Revolución de Mayo*, we referred to the beginnings of militarisation in Argentinian society.

The Austrian sociologist, Otto Baur, used to say that countries are 'solidified histories'. In general, historians in Argentina do not 'make History' just to learn about the past but to understand the present a little better; to try to answer some of the questions we all ask ourselves at some stage in life, not only as individuals but as a community. We all ask ourselves where we come from, where we are going, who we are, why we are here, why certain things happen to us, why we are different from others, what our identity is, what we can do, what our talents are, and so on and so on.

Although History does not answer all of these questions (or if it does, it does not give us a full answer to all of them) it does help us in some way to see where we stand and herein lies its usefulness. When all is said and done the historian does not gaze into a crystal ball. But, insofar as he can get an overview of the phenomena he is looking at, he is in a better position to sound the alarm.

In this respect, when depicting the democratic experience the country underwent between the Sáenz Peña Law in 1912 and 1930 when it came to such a rude end, one cannot help pondering how fragile our political system is and how impatience has so often got in the way of improving and enriching it.

CHAPTER IX THE 1930 REVOLUTION

The 1930 Revolution was a watershed in Argentina's constitutional history. This was the first time an elected government had been overthrown by a military coup or, to call it by its real name, a civilian-military coup. Myself, I think it was catastrophic both because of what it left in its wake and the windows of opportunity it closed. I realise that by making this statement I am in a way taking sides, but a historian does not have to abdicate his values, the backbone of his beliefs, his stance towards his country and the world.

THE PLEBISCITE

When I say that the revolution of September 6 was a catastrophe for the institutions, I am simply stating my scale of values regarding Argentina. Even if it was a catastrophe, a revolution always has its causes and we need to examine them. Our attention must accordingly turn back a couple of years to 1928, the year of the election long remembered as "the plebiscite", when Hipólito Yrigoyen was elected for the second time.

In these elections two clear-cut political factions became visible: those who adhered to everything Yrigoyen stood for and those who rejected him. Yrigoyen was the unchallenged leader of the Radicals though the party had split three or four years earlier. One group was called "Antipersonalist" and was made up of those who attacked Yrigoyen's allegedly personalist methods. It would nowadays be described as centre-right.

Antipersonalism's centre-right leanings are proved by the fact that in 1928 the faction was openly supported by conservative parties all over the country who saw in the Melo-Gallo ticket the opportunity to bar Yrigoyen from a second term in office. The head of the traditional wing of the *UCR* still won hands down: eight hundred and forty thousand votes as against the four hundred and sixty thousand of all his opponents put together.

Paradoxically, Yrigoyen's landslide victory goaded the opposition into seeking a return to power through methods other than elections. It also lulled the *Yrigoyenistas* into a dangerous false sense of security: they regarded the "plebiscite" as a true statement of national belief in Yrigoyen and a justification of any future mistakes or omissions because results were so overwhelming that people's allegiances seemed unlikely to change. This provides us with a first hint at why the 1930 revolution was staged: the Conservatives were deeply disappointed at the election results, which they saw as Argentina leaping into the void.

Secondly, in 1930 Argentina was suffering the backlash of a world crisis that had begun with the Wall Street crash of 1929. Many governments took measures such as currency and customs controls geared to curbing previously unrestricted international trade in order to save their economies from catastrophe. Let us not forget that Argentina had until then been strictly an exporter of staple goods with a very rudimentary industrial base, and as a result its economy was vulnerable to the vagaries of international finance. In 1929 Argentinian exports fell drastically below previous levels.

Thirdly, 1930 was a unique time in world history since it saw the rise of political systems opposed to the traditional liberal democracy that had prevailed in Europe and most civilised countries until World War I. Fascism had imposed order in Italy since 1923 and subsequently endeavoured to turn it into a world power. The charismatic figure of Mussolini won admirers the world over, even among the likes of Churchill who was eventually to become Italy's enemy. In Spain, Fascism took the shape of Primo de Rivera.

On the other hand, there was the Bolshevik regime that had seized power in 1917 and which, under Stalin's iron rule, was after 1925 attempting full-scale industrialisation (with apparent success according to his followers' claims the world around). Apart from the crisis that had shaken the US and apparently jeopardised the entire capitalist system, there were several military coups in Latin America that toppled some relatively democratic civilian governments.

A UNIQUE MOMENT

Meanwhile, Argentinian politics was in the doldrums. The purpose of Yrigoyen's first government seemed to have lost its way. It had been a peaceful, top-down revolution that had attempted to distribute wealth more equally and strengthen the State's leverage in the arbitration of opposing social interests; to create a more just society and implement more nationally-oriented economic policies. But by now Yrigoyen was beginning to look like an ageing statesman losing his grip. Public administration too was slowly grinding to a halt.

Anyway, one of the mysteries of this period is why the Argentinian upper classes hated Yrigoyen so much that they brought down traditional legalistic conservatism and embarked on a revolution, when the truth of the matter is that Yrigoyen never attacked the economic bastions of the 'oligarchs', and went out of his way to respect their life-style. Nevertheless, hatred of Yrigoyen was quite tangible in those days. It was vented in newspapers, magazines and books; Yrigoyen took the blame for everything. But the grudges against him were non-specific and reveal the prejudices of the upper classes. One cannot therefore help wondering how such a bold revolution could have been embarked upon on the basis of mere allegations.

There is an interesting book by Martín Aldao that reflects the tone of the times very well. Aldao was a gentleman from a very old family in Santa Fe and lived in Paris for thirty or forty years. He was well-known in the French community and had the bright idea of keeping a diary. In it he wrote about his experiences, the books he read, the artistic landmarks he witnessed, and his conversations with the most prominent men in the Argentinian community in France. Here is a précis of his diary from around 1928 to 1932 which includes the entire sequence of events leading up to the revolution on September 6 and its aftermath. From his conversations with personalities such as Marcelo T. de Alvear, Fernando Saguier and other prominent Argentinians, both resident and visiting, it is clear how inconsistent the rumours were. Nevertheless, they do point to the weightiest arguments against Yrigoyen: "He's gaga. He's paralysing the entire civil service because he won't sign. He's surrounded by stalwarts. He'll govern with any old Tom, Dick and Harry."

It is interesting that as from late 1929 or early 1930, Aldao quite matter-of-factly records the possibility of a rebellion against Yrigoyen. He also names names: it was to be headed by General Justo or General Uriburu. This bespeaks a lack of responsibility in the handling of these affairs, but at the same time one has to admit that the Radicals remained very passive and lacked the initiative to face up to or put an end to the seemingly inexorable turn things had started taking in June or July 1930. The 1928 victory (the celebrated "plebiscite"), had silenced any concern or criticism. Because of vested election interests the Radicals presented candidates in March 1930 who already had a seat. They were all duly re-elected, something quite at odds with what Radicalism and Yrigoyen had stood for a few years earlier.

OUTBREAKS OF VIOLENCE

In November 1929, for the first time in recent memory, a macabre event took place: the assassination of the leader Carlos Washington Lencinas in Mendoza. Lencinas was a Radical dissident and had taken a more than progressive stance towards economic and social issues. The Lencinas family in Mendoza and the Cantoni family in San Juan were almost caricatures of Radicalism: overly populist and generous in thought and deed. Their stance was similar to Peronism's later: aggression towards anything to do with capital and business, support of the workers and progressive legislation such as allowing women to vote in San Juan in the 1928 provincial elections. Yet a sense of impending violence against the opposition was in the air.

The young Carlos Washington Lencinas was the son of the first Radical governor of Mendoza, Lencinas the gaucho. (Carlos Washington himself was referred to as *gauchito* Lencinas, or 'gaucho junior'.) After waging bloody campaigns against Yrigoyen, he arrived in Mendoza in November 1929 and was assassinated by a lowly fellow countryman who supported Yrigoyen. A political motive was immediately attributed to the crime and tempers rose throughout Argentina. Yrigoyen was promptly accused of having encouraged the assassination of Lencinas, a barbaric act from any angle you care to look at it.

In fact, the situation in the Cuyo region reflected its peculiar circumstances; circumstances which had driven federal forces to intervene in San Juan and Mendoza before Yrigoyen ever came to power. But the intervening forces had also dealt extremely violently with matters and resistance was shown by supporters of both Lencinas and Cantoni. The crime itself, though apparently only an event of local importance, had nation-wide repercussions.

A month later more blood was spilled: an obscure, possibly slightly deranged, anarchist sympathiser fired shots at Yrigoyen's car as he left his house on his way to Government House. The potential assassin was immediately shot dead by Yrigoyen's armed guards but the event lent credence to a series of criticisms of the president, who used not to need an escort and now surrounded himself with armed policemen who shot to kill. These events began to create an ominous, intimidating atmosphere and, although not broadcast nation-wide, they were nevertheless skilfully exploited by the press and opposition in the national elections of March 1930.

STRANGE ELECTIONS

These elections ended up as a kind of draw. The eight hundred thousand votes cast for Radicalism in 1928 dropped to six hundred thousand in 1930, while votes for the opposition, with around four hundred thousand in 1928, climbed to the same number. But the unprecedented event from an electoral point of view was that in the Federal Capital, in Buenos Aires, the Radicals lost to a minority faction of a minority party. The Independent Socialist Party was a dissident wing of the traditional Socialist Party. They were more adamantly anti-Yrigoyen than the Socialist Party and in time formed an alliance with conservative forces to create what later came to be known as the *Concordancia*.

The Radicals' defeat in Buenos Aires at the hands of such a makeshift party was a warning. After that the possibility of a military conspiracy, which had been in the air a couple of years earlier at the time of Yrigoyen's victory, began to be taken seriously. In those days the money was firmly on General Agustín P. Justo, Alvear's War Minister, but in light of Yrigoyen's recent triumph in the plebiscite, the general believed that any revolutionary action would have been overruled. By 1930 things had changed and the wheels of conspiracy began to roll. They were driven by a man who had been a conservative deputy back in 1913, the Salta-born General José Félix Uriburu.

Uriburu was a pro-German surrounded by youth groups with little political but some intellectual clout, which stemmed from a daily called *La Nueva República* (The New Republic). These group gave Italian fascism an Argentinian face and proclaimed the irrelevance of democracy in the quest for the common good. It cast doubt on the validity of elections claiming that there was no reason why majorities had to be in the right. More than anything it tried to undermine the party political system and proposed corporate constitutional reforms.

THE CONSPIRACY

Uriburu was a sincere, well-intentioned man but he was intellectually rather blinkered. He had allowed himself to get embroiled with these almost exclusively Conservative youths (many of whom, such as Ernesto Palacios or the Irazusta brothers, were brilliant thinkers), and as a result became a potential leader of the conspiracy. He had served until 1928 and carried prestige in the Army. He began talking to a lot of people about a revolution that, in his opinion, was to herald a new era in the development of the country's institutions, as well as reform of the Constitution, abolition of the Sáenz Peña Law and the creation of a sort of Chamber of Italian-style *Fasci* or Corporations that would replace Congress.

Not long afterwards, General Justo hatched his own conspiracy with the intention of blocking Uriburu's proposals for constitutional reform. Justo was surrounded by politicians of the old school, consisting mainly of Conservatives, Antipersonalists (or anti-Yrigoyen Radicals) and Independent Socialists. He felt Yrigoyen had to be deposed because he no longer had a firm grip on the helm of the State. This he felt would pave the way for elections and allow the front defeated in 1928 to take power by relatively constitutional means. It is worth underlining the fact that, although at this time the conspirators did not engage in open argument, they were in fact being led in two quite divergent directions.

In the public arena, the conspiracy ran parallel to a whole series of public demonstrations by the opposition parties both in Congress and on the streets. All the members of the opposition joined forces in a kind of united front and staged thrilling public events in theatres and squares while intensifying their criticism of the regime. The opposition controlled much of the media, which allowed them to constantly drum their accusations into the public, the results of which became clear in August 1930.

When the time for revolution is ripe governments generally take action which the opposition reacts to thus creating a counterpoint of opposition and government which reaches a climax in the revolution itself. The curious thing in this case was that the government did nothing at all apart from the odd trivial decree or administrative act such as appointing a president of the Supreme Court. Where in 1955 there were actions from Perón's government which in turn provoked reactions that culminated in the revolution of September 16, none of this occurred in 1930.

The Radical government just sat there like some ventriloquist's dummy and did not react to the volley of blows raining down on them. Their only retort came towards the end of August 1930 in the form of a handful of pro-government demonstrations by a rather obscure organisation called the Radical Clan. This group consisted of the rank and file of the local Radical branches, who paraded through the centre of Buenos Aires shouting long live Yrigoyen and down with his opponents. There were no serious repercussions or even casualties, despite a few shots being fired.

The conspiracy gathered momentum in the press with predictions about when the revolution would break out. In August and early September 1930 some newspapers, notably *Crítca* and *La Razón*, were saying the most appalling things about the president. If you compare these ferocious verbal onslaughts to electoral campaigns or present-day allegations from the opposition, the extent to which Argentinian political manners have improved becomes clear. They would even pick on Yrigoyen's private personality and reach the heights of obscenity without the government so much as batting an eyelid.

In early September the War Minister resigned, unable to contain the conspiracy as there was also conniving within the government. On September 4 there was a demonstration in which the first long-awaited victim, a student by all accounts, died in a shoot-out. Though later it was confirmed that he was a actually banker, the students of Buenos Aires came out on strike and declared war on the government. On September 6, General Uriburu advanced on Buenos Aires with a highly vulnerable short column of cadets from the Military College.

But the atmosphere was such that he had no chance of meeting with any resistance. The ailing Yrigoyen had handed over command to his vice-president, Enrique Martínez. This gesture was not good enough. Nothing less than Yrigoyen's resignation would do and eventually Uriburu reached Government House after a shoot-out in the Plaza del Congreso. There he forced the vice-president to resign and took charge of the de facto government.

LIMITED ELECTIONS

What happened next gives us a taste of what would take place later in the 30s. Uriburu tried to put his corporate plans into action, but he could not stir up public opinion. Moreover, Justo flatly refused to cooperate and even attempted, unsuccessfully as it turned out, to set up a confederation of sorts to strengthen his hand. In the end, Uriburu had to give in to the conservatives, who were his only support. On the advice of his Interior Minister, elections were called in Buenos Aires Province with the intention of gradually doing the same elsewhere, the process culminating with the announcement of a new president.

But on April 5 1931 Radicalism unexpectedly triumphed in Buenos Aires Province and things began to get complicated for Uriburu. From the moment the Radicals were discovered to still be the majority party (despite their loss of prestige, despite Yrigoyen being in jail and the fact that many of its leaders were either absent or also in jail) Uriburu had to look for other methods. The one he hit upon involved rigging an election and poisoning the air for the rest of the decade: he vetoed the Radical ticket of Marcelo de Alvear and Adolfo Güemes in September 1931.

Faced with this veto, the Radicals once again abstained. The forces supporting the provisional government comprised the old Conservatives (who, under the name of the National Democratic Party, managed to unite into a single national party for the first time since the Sáenz Peña Law had been passed), the Antipersonalist wing of Radicalism and the Independent Socialists in Buenos Aires. Their ticket was Justo-Roca, and Justo-Matienzo (Justo-Roca backed by the Conservatives and Justo-Matienzo by the Antipersonalists). The remainder, who were neither Radicals nor Conservatives (in other words, the traditional socialists, progressive democrats and minor provincial parties) formed the Civilian Alliance, whose candidates were Lisandro de la Torre (Progressive Democrat) and Nicolás Repetto (Socialist).

In the elections the provincial Conservative party machinery inevitably prevailed over the civilian alliances, who only won the Federal Capital and Santa Fe, where the Progressive Democrat Party had a strong foothold. The National Congress assembled in December 1931 and endorsed the elections despite protests from the Radicals. On 20 February 1932 Uriburu handed the presidency over to General Agustín P. Justo.

CONSEQUENCES

In short, in September 1930, for the first time in Argentina's constitutional history, a military coup unseated a constitutional government. Subsequently a system of election fraud and constitutional and judicial violation was established. This was what permitted the *Concordancia* to foist its candidates on the public until 1943.

Behind all this (which on the surface seems like just another Latin American military coup) lies the eagerness with which

Argentina's ruling classes seized power to deal with the crisis without being in the least affected by it. By taking power these classes arranged things in such a way that the effects of the crisis facing Argentina did not damage their basic interests, but were evenly distributed over the population as a whole.

Another consequence of the revolution of September 6 was the reconstruction of the Radical Party, which put aside its old Antipersonalist and Yrigoyenist differences and united under Alvear. Yrigoyen, who had been detained on Martín García Island, was pardoned by the provisional government and returned to Buenos Aires. He did not however resume the leadership of his party but limited himself to giving his blessing to his chosen disciple, Marcelo T. de Alvear, the new Radical leader.

Many things changed in Argentina after 1930, most of them for the worse. Sixteen years later, the great Conservative leader from Córdoba, José Aguirre Cámara, spoke these words to his party's national committee: "In 1930 we committed a grave error out of our impatience, our love of power, our inexperience, for whatever reason. We paved the way for military uprisings and we forgot our great Conservative tradition. From that moment on, we Conservatives have been responsible for everything that has happened in our country up to the present day. We are guilty." A few years after these words, Perón was to say: "I was very young when I witnessed the fall of Yrigoyen; and I saw him go under in a wave of calumny and insults that his government was powerless to resist. This will not happen to me..." Both men felt it necessary to make a statement of personal guilt at the part they played in the 1930 revolution.

The fact is that after 1930 the events of September 6 were remembered with some ceremony to begin with, then with ever-growing silence until in the end they have been completely forgotten. Nowadays nobody remembers the date with any certainty: there exists a vague idea that it was a despicable moment in Argentina's institutional history. It paved the way for further breaches of the Constitution, and began a decade of supremacy for the traditional classes, whose self-seeking class-consciousness and lack of concern for the common good signalled a step backwards to Argentina's past.

CHAPTER X THE NINETEEN THIRTIES

The name "década del 30" *in Argentinian Spanish does not strictly refer to a chronological period. Politically speaking, the decade begins in February 1932, when Agustín P. Justo took office, and finishes in 1943 with the overthrow of Ramón S. Castillo's Conservative government.*

In history as in life, things are all going on at once: one should bear in mind that political issues are simultaneous with economic processes and cultural events, even though it may be necessary to carve history up into distinct episodes for the sake of comprehensibility. Therefore, I would like to outline the historical framework of what was happening in the world at large during this period. For seldom in contemporary history has there been a decade so grimly portentous as the 1930s.

GRIM OMENS

In 1933 Hitler seized power in Germany. His racist, nationalist and militaristic policies led him to occupy the Ruhr, engulf Austria, invade the Sudetenland (and subsequently the whole of Czechoslovakia) and eventually Poland in September 1939, which triggered the Second World War.

Events in the Soviet Union, although generally welcomed by progressive elements in the West (Argentina included), nevertheless concealed a grim truth for humankind, which only gradually came to light. The idea of a classless society was tantalising: a society in which money and privilege would not matter, and where everyone would work towards a better standard of living. But this was accompanied by terrible internal repression: almost ten million peasants opposed to agricultural policy were liquidated; there were swingeing trials in Moscow, where the most senior veteran leaders of the Bolshevik revolution confessed to their 'crimes' (treason against Mother Russia, conspiracy to kill Stalin). But this only came to light later. At the time the Soviet Union seemed to be conducting a huge experiment as an alternative to capitalism, which was apparently on the verge of bankruptcy.

In the United States there were twenty million unemployed and much the same situation existed in England and France. This led to rioting which, if not threatening to destabilise the system completely, nevertheless managed to spread alarm among its leaders. The United States replaced its traditionally liberal policies with large-scale public works to alleviate unemployment. With hindsight, Roosevelt's New Deal seems not to have been as instrumental in overcoming the crisis as it was in imbuing the American people with a new feeling of confidence.

Things were not well with the world. Totalitarianism made headway and democracy was called into question. Fierce armed confrontation was a common occurrence: Japan's invasion of China for example, or the Spanish Civil War, which broke out in July 1936 and lasted until May 1939. This prelude to the Second World War rocked Argentinian society.

There were many reasons why the Spanish Civil War affected Argentina so deeply. First and foremost of these was that the Spanish community was so large. Today only the great-grandchildren are left but at the time there were many Spanish parents and grandparents, and all of them took sides over events in the Peninsula. Moreover commercial and economic ties were much deeper than now exist between the two countries: Argentinians ate Spanish sardines, drank Spanish cider and washed with Spanish soap. There were large Spanish public service companies like the one that built Line D of the underground from Plaza de Mayo to the Pacífico Bridge in Buenos Aires; or the CHADE (Hispano-Argentinian Electricity Company), whose headquarters were in Barcelona.

But quite apart from its ties with Spain, Argentinian society was so deeply affected because the values at stake were so closely related to its own. The upheavals of the Spanish Civil War and later the Second World War shook Argentinian society awake. Our country had up until then been engrossed in its own affairs, a stranger to what was going on in the outside world. After the war all this changed.

JUSTO

The thirties began with Agustín P. Justo's dubious victory in the 1931 elections. The election ban on the Radical party involved an implicit fraud which let the *Concordancia* (literally, Concordance or Agreement) into power. The *Concordancia* was a loose coalition of traditional Conservatives, Antipersonalists and Independent Socialists that had prevailed in the Federal Capital in 1930.

Justo, the new Antipersonalist Radical president, had not the slightest charisma but he did have political cunning and had found a way to raise support. He was a professional soldier and had been Alvear's war minister. On top of this he was a civil engineer, a fact played on during the electoral campaign to show that he was not a military president but a man who combined military activity with a civilian profession.

Justo was booed wherever he went. His is perhaps the only case of a president who, on the occasion of a big race at the Palermo racecourse, actually gave himself the satisfaction of using a certain gesture of the forearm at the crowd. But booed or not Justo did get things done: his government produced a good many public works and it is to him that we owe the first network of paved roads in Argentina. The roads from Buenos Aires to Mar del Plata, Mendoza (via Río Cuarto) and Córdoba (via Rosario) are all General Justo's doing. During his government the Highway Administration Law, which put five cents on the price of petrol, was passed and the revenue channelled into building paved roads.

Although regarding himself as an Antipersonalist Radical, in his actions Justo was a Conservative. He believed in the thinking that had made the nation prosper in recent decades: close association with

Britain, the safeguarding of British capital invested in Argentina and commercial ties between Argentina and Britain. But when it came to planning the roads, Justo decided that they would run parallel to the railways and thus helped to fan competition between the British-owned railways and an increasingly significant fleet of lorries. Road transport was no quicker or safer than the railways but it did have cheaper tariffs.

The early years of Justo's government were smoothed by the Radical Party's policy of abstention. After being banned from the 1931 elections, some Radical leaders encouraged various attempts at revolution (which invariably failed) while sheltering under the abstention policy. They had no way out: abstention from elections meant being sidelined while other parties were playing by the *Concordancia*'s rules. Thanks to the gap left by the Radicals, the Socialist Party had fifty odd deputies in Congress, a figure they were never to reach again.

ELECTION FRAUD

In 1935 the Radical Party decided to lift its abstention policy. From then on, vote rigging, the most conspicuous and least justifiable blot on the decade, began to be practised on a grand scale. If not directly organised by them, then the government certainly did more than just turn a blind eye to it.

It basically involved intimidating opposition voters into not voting, or threatening polling clerks (on occasion with weapons) so that they would leave proceedings to supporters of the ruling party, who were then free to fill the ballot boxes with their own votes. Another bogus government practise was allowing people to vote freely as in the past and then switching ballot boxes.

The fraud included anything from scheming to outright acts of aggression. In the Radical Party's often armed efforts to clean up voting procedures many died in the ensuing shootings. In 1935 Amadeo Sabatini won in Córdoba after eight or nine of his men died in a clash with Conservative thugs. The same happened in Mendoza, where the governing party killed the Radical branch president, Dr. Martons. In Santa Fe Province General Risso Patrón was killed. In Buenos Aires Province, the scene of the worst excesses, events were of almost epic proportions. Juan Maciel, the Radical leader in Tres Arroyos, knowing that rigging was taking place in the Coronel Dorrego ward on the day of Ortiz's election (against the Radical Alvear) went out to stop it and died in a hail of bullets in the town square. So far the full story of this distressingly intricate struggle has not been told.

Unfortunately, the Radical Party itself was no angel when it came to vote rigging. In the late thirties and early forties there were instances of cheating in the Radical Party's internal elections. A black stain was spreading across Argentina. Rigging elections was the only way for the minority *Concordancia* coalition to hold on to power against the Radicals.

The question of election fraud rightly belongs to political philosophy. What kind of pressure and how much should a government bring to bear in order to hold on to power? "Man's first care is to look after his own hide," says the gaucho, Martin Fierro. It could also be said that the first duty of a political leader in government is to stay in government. But what limits should be placed on the expedients he can use? The Conservatives and their Antipersonalist allies did not bother to ask themselves this question. They did what they felt they had to wherever necessary, the only exception being the Federal Capital of Buenos Aires.

Election fraud is the defining factor in Argentinian politics in the thirties, which deserve their nickname of the *década infame* or "despicable decade" as it was dubbed by a nationalist journalist. Although the label cannot be applied to every aspect of government action, it can be applied to the political fringes. Here 'infamy' was not only to do with rigging votes and stealing ballot boxes but also with the deep scepticism that had spread through Argentinian society about the validity of democracy.

The spectacle of totalitarianism making headway in Europe and of a democratic system at home based on election fraud, cheating, lies and hypocrisy (there was always a spokesman to hand who denied any involvement) brought about the decline of democracy and left it defenceless when in 1943 President Ramón Castillo's government, which was at least elected according to the constitution, was defeated.

ORTIZ

When Justo reached the end of his term, an attempt was made to breathe new life into the Conservative-Antipersonalist alliance (the Independent Socialists were by this time out of the picture). Roberto Ortiz was secretly chosen as the *Concordancia*'s candidate. The Radical Party, which had by now joined the fold, put forward Marcelo de Alvear whose distinguished presidency in the previous decade was still strong in people's memories. The elections were once again rigged and Ortiz elected. However, the new president realised that things could not go on like this forever.

Ortiz was a sincere democrat who did his apprenticeship in the ranks of the Radical Party, went on to become an active Antipersonalist and finally became a minister in the Justo government. He felt that repeated vote rigging was damaging for the country and set about eradicating it. He did so by boldly severing his ties with those who had raised him to power. But bad luck and bad health let him down. Ortiz was a diabetic. Although he heroically fought his disease, he was not able to control it entirely and in July 1940 a lesion on the retina left him practically blind. He asked for leave and effectively ended his presidency (though in formal terms he continued to hold office). The Conservative vice-president and Ortiz's running partner, Castillo, took the reins of government.

Like Justo, Castillo believed it was madness to let the Radicals win the elections and continued to back fraudulent practices. Perhaps the most outrageous moment came in December 1941 when Rodolfo Moreno was elected governor of Buenos Aires on the back of vote rigging on a gigantic scale. It was condemned by all the newspapers of the day but the story was eclipsed to some extent by the news that Japan was bombing Pearl Harbour on the very day the fraud was committed. (People joked that the attack was an agreement between

Moreno, an ex-ambassador to Japan, and Tokyo.) After these elections Castillo steered things in such a way as to ensure that any future president would be a true blue Conservative.

THE CRISIS

The economic crisis that ravaged the country in the thirties was at its height when Justo came to power in 1932. It involved a painful international readjustment that could only be accomplished by enforcing stringent customs checks and barriers, which in turn began to interfere with international trade. Individual countries tried to protect their economies with new regulations that disrupted previously unrestricted trade between countries. The crisis brought on a sharp drop in the price of raw materials exported by Argentina: things like meat, wool, wheat, oil-based products and tannin. When its income fell the government could perform fewer public works and the state apparatus became less efficient.

The Conservative government announced that they had to protect genuine sources of wealth in order to tackle the crisis and reconstruct the economy, and that in the face of this one should not worry too much about people suffering. As it happened, this wealth belonged to the men who were in the government, the big cattle-breeders and farm-owners, the people associated with the international meat trade and this was of pivotal importance in overcoming the crisis.

A second important element was vigorous State intervention in the economy in the shape of the Central Bank, which was set up to regulate all aspects of foreign exchange and financial concerns. It was founded as a group of public and private banks who would be in charge of managing banking policy. Apart from this, an exchange control mechanism was established and a tight rein kept on credit policy. This meant State influence through the Central Bank on a previously unrestricted banking and financial system. However, Raúl Prebisch, the man at the helm, acted prudently and the Central Bank's considerable moderating influence was one of the factors that allowed the crisis to be overcome relatively quickly. These men, whose philosophy was to safeguard genuine sources of wealth, opted neither for a policy of inflation or devaluation. A peso was hard won but once you earned it you could rest assured that it would be worth the same in five or ten years, a fact that was instrumental in holding back the crisis.

Thirdly, the crisis was surmounted by setting up various regulatory bodies. In other words, despite the government's Conservative colours, State interventionism during the 30s was absolute. This was a stance which took its theory from old-style Liberalism; nevertheless, especially under Federico Pinedo's economic policy, the Conservatives did not hesitate to intervene forcefully in the production of raw materials. Their idea was that only regulation of production would keep prices at a level profitable for producers. Wine was poured away in Mendoza, farmland was reduced and production was entrusted with the job of keeping agricultural and livestock producers afloat: there were Meat Regulating Boards, Corn Regulating Boards, Wheat Regulating Boards, Cotton Regulating Boards, Wine Regulating Boards, you name it. The same kind of thing was happening elsewhere. In Brazil coffee was being thrown into the sea by the sackful so that overproduction would not bring down international prices.

The crisis was harsh and made itself felt especially in the mass of the population: there was high unemployment; the railway unions were forced to accept pay cuts from English companies; and civil servants went for long periods without being paid. The schoolteachers in Santiago del Estero and Corrientes were the prime example of unpaid civil servants and went without their wage packets for two or three years. The popular music of the day reflected the situation in lines like "where there's the odd peso, old Gómez, they've rubbed it away with old pummice..." *Rancheras* like this one sent shock waves through the middle and upper middle classes. Some prominent families had to sell their residences, which were acquired by foreign embassies, or by the State to use as government offices, and this has at least preserved some fine architectural specimens in Buenos Aires.

Nevertheless, despite the sacrifice of the working classes and high unemployment, the crisis (which, they say, found its own solutions) did have some positive effects. The drop in agricultural and livestock prices pushed unemployment in rural areas up to very high levels and as a result many rural workers moved to the big cities. This, added to the difficulty of importing certain types of commodities, created thousands of small businesses, workshops, textile mills, chemical laboratories and pharmacies based on cheap labour from rural areas. A fairly rudimentary national industry began to take shape: its products were not cheap but it laid the foundations of the light industry whose heyday would come in the 40s.

This emergent industrial activity was accompanied by the gradual influx of country-dwellers into the cities. Buenos Aires, La Plata, Rosario were all places where those from the rural areas could find regular wages a better quality of life, better housing and social connections. A class began to emerge that had nothing to do with Socialist or Communist affiliated union members. These people were different and did not feel bound by any political loyalties.

When times are bad workers do not dare to go on strike but when things get a little better, relations between management and workers begin to find their natural level. Around 1935 the crisis began to subside and a period of major strikes set in. In this year, one construction workers strike in Buenos Aires lasted almost six months and finished with a settlement that suited everybody, as strikes usually do.

THE TREATY

This crisis, weathered with such hardships, had one extremely important dimension to it, namely the reaffirmation of the traditional pro-British philosophy of Argentinian business, the most important expression of which was the Roca-Runciman Pact signed in 1933. The crisis had affected Argentina's major producers, above all the big ranch-owners and cattle-breeders. Frozen meat, the most advanced product of Argentinian ranching, was particularly hard hit.

The delegation Argentina sent for talks in Britain was headed by Vice-President Julio Roca, who after some difficult negotiating signed the so-called Roca-Runciman Treaty. This agreement is highly complex and whole libraries have been written for and against it. I shall greatly simplify the treaty by saying that it consisted of a British guarantee to continue buying refrigerated meat in the same quantities on average as in the 1920s. In fact the figure was a little below this average but it did insure constant trade for cattle-breeders and ranch-owners in Argentina.

In exchange Argentina pledged "benevolent treatment" of British capital and this was translated into a foreign exchange mechanism that favoured British companies sending their earnings to head office. Another result of the pledge was an attempt to coordinate transport in Argentina in order to stop competition from lorries and buses, which were ruining the English railways and tramways.

The most striking thing about the Roca-Runciman Treaty was Roca's distinctly unhappy words expressing what was actually a very intelligent stance for Argentina to strike. Roca said that owing to the extent of Britain's interests in Argentina, our country could be considered just another British colony. His sentiments caused a sensation when they were communicated to Buenos Aires. Roca was bitterly criticised but what he was driving at was that, in the face of a world crisis and following other countries' examples, Britain had drawn up the Ottawa Treaty whereby it gave preferential treatment to its own territories: Canadian meat, Australian wool and textiles from India would all therefore receive preferential treatment in the British marketplace over the same products from other countries.

Great Britain wanted to keep up its empire, which was maintained not only through loyalty to the Crown but also commercial ties. These allowed British markets with their great purchasing power to continuing importing products from British territories. According to the Argentinian government Argentina, which had the most significant quantity of investments and close commercial ties with Britain, should have received the same preferential treatment that Britain gave its territories.

This encouraged Argentinian negotiators to go to London to try, under the terms of the treaty, to secure protection for a genuine source of wealth such as refrigerated meat exports, in exchange for which they promised to protect British capital at home. Nothing definite came of these negotiations because shortly after they began the Second World War broke out and relations between Argentina and Britain altered completely.

The crisis was ridden out and by 1935 or 1936 Argentina had reverted to the dynamics of the twenties, with the additional income of foreign capital fleeing Europe in alarm at Hitler's warmongering, Mussolini's claims, the Soviet enigma and the weakness of France and England. By this time war seemed almost inevitable and so it was. The foreign capital coming into Argentina, some of which was Jewish, helped to revitalise the economy.

SOCIETY

The 1930s was an interesting time for Argentinian society. These are the days of *Sur* (South) founded in 1931 by Victoria Ocampo, an Argentinian Gertrude Stein. This cultural review was a window on the outside world and dragged us from our cultural self-absorption. It is when Jorge Luis Borges began publishing his *Historia universal de la infamia* (Universal History of Infamy) and a few stories in the daily newspaper, *Crítica*. Eduardo Mallea too was publishing his great works, novels like *La bahía de silencio* (The Bay of Silence) for example. The poet and prose writer Leopoldo Lugones committed suicide on 20 February 1938, the same day Roberto Ortiz took office. The poetess Alfonsina Storni also took her own life. Carlos Gardel had already died in 1935 in a plane crash in Medellín, Colombia, though in those days he was not the idol he has since become. Serious tango orchestras had begun to spring up everywhere. There was an extremely significant artistic movement and great freedom of expression: pluralism and tolerance of any intellectual expression, even the most dissident, was the order of the day.

The exception to the rule was a law passed in Justo's presidency and pushed through by Matías Sánchez Sorondo, a Conservative senator for Buenos Aires Province; however, apart from declaring the Communist Party illegal, it did not have any great impact. The Communist Party were old hands at living as outlaws and, since they were also very low in numbers, Sorondo's law did not effectively signal a backwards step in our traditional respect for freedom of expression.

The stigma of fraud went beyond mere politics to contaminate other aspects of Argentinian life. Some episodes from the 30s cast serious doubt on the credibility of democracy. There was some shady dealing which we could now look back on with a smile, but at the time it rocked the foundations of society and emboldened those who were questioning democracy. They contended that a fraudulent system did not have the capacity to prevent this kind of scamming.

The CHADE deal was the first in which a transnational company bought out a legislative organisation for commercial ends. The CHADE supplied electricity to Buenos Aires but their concession was about to expire. Consequently, they began bribing people left, right and centre, councillors and journalists, managers and senior government officials, in order to get the concession deadline extended to the end of the century.

Alvear himself had a hand in the affair. Although not actually taking any bribes, he nevertheless advised Radical councillors to vote in line with the CHADE's request. Complaints were lodged at the time (though no proof was found) and subsequently, after the 1943 revolution, the scandal was investigated in depth. The conclusions of the investigation were later destroyed on Perón's orders but a few copies were saved and they show the sophistication of the CHADE's radio-controlled operation from Brussels, where the company had its head office. They also show the complicity of senior figures in Argentinian life.

Another shady deal which took place in 1940, around the time of Ortiz's request for sick leave, involved the land in El Palomar in Greater Buenos Aires. The War Minister wanted to buy this land for the military academy. A band of wheeler-dealers that included deputies bought the land from some old women, sold it to the State at a profit and pocketed the difference. The shocking thing is that the old women sold the land to these barefaced opportunists, who there and then sold it to the Government; in the same notary's office, on the same day! There was an inquiry; it immediately became flagrantly obvious who was to blame for the ill-concealed scam and, surprise surprise, a Radical deputy who had received ten thousand pesos shot himself. People were still sensitive about these kinds of gaffs...

A GOOD DECADE?

All in all, however, except for the stigma of fraud that cast its shadow over everything, it was a good decade once the worst years were over. During the crisis people were pessimistic because Argentina had never been through anything like it since 1890. But 1890 was nearly half a century in the past and, even in crisis, the tone of Argentinians fairly oozed with conviction: "God is a *criollo* and a couple of good harvests will see things right." Prosperity was after all Argentina's destiny!

But this was not to be and the crisis hit people very hard indeed. When it gradually began to abate, the country's jubilant optimism returned and people carried on with their socially stratified lives as conventionally and misoneistically as ever. Nevertheless, these years did preserve some of the best features of the past: there was great social fluidity; both foreigners and wannabes were welcomed with open arms. There was plenty of work but also time for amusement; people had just the one job (nobody dreamt of holding down more than one), had lunch at home and slept a siesta before going back to the daily grind. One can look on this decade with a certain nostalgia.

There were a handful of important political parties: the Radicals, who thought of themselves as the majority party (led at the time by Marcelo de Alvear, a man respected by everyone); the Conservatives, who had only united in 1931 but had competent senior politicians; the Socialists, whose headquarters, though limited to the Federal Capital, contained men of the first rank (Alfredo Palacios, Enrique Dickman, Nicolás Repetto, Mario Bravo); and the handful of Progressive Democrats from Santa Fe, who managed to form a government under Luciano Molinas between 1932 and 1935, in which Justo's intervention was one of the most unjustifiable events of the decade.

One might have expected civic practices to improve, as well as greater participation from non-Conservative forces who could represent at least some of the claims of the rest of the population. But this did not happen: the fraudulent practices, stubbornness and blindness of the ruling classes prevented it. The effects of their actions would make themselves felt in 1943, the year which really marks the end of the 30s.

CHAPTER XI THE 1943 REVOLUTION

The so-called "Revolution" of 1943 came like lightning on a fine day. One morning the city's inhabitants awoke to the news that troops from the army's Campo de Mayo training camp had marched on Government House in the Plaza de Mayo. President Castillo was on his way to Colonia in Uruguay and the Conservative government had been overthrown. Yet the coup was perfectly predictable and even inevitable. This may seem like a contradiction in terms but, although the coup was sparked off by a quite absurdly commonplace incident, it was consistent with background events that had been developing for some years. With hindsight these are more clearly visible than at the time.

TOTALITARIANISM

In order to understand these events, one must bear in mind the impetus of totalitarianism, which after 1933 made political and military gains and which at the time practically governed European life. From a historical perspective, by mid-1943 the war had turned around and an Allied victory was inevitable. In late 1942 the first great defeat of the totalitarian regimes had taken place, the Battle of Stalingrad, where the Germans lost more than 600,000 men and could no longer reach the Suez Canal. The war being waged between Japan and the United States in the Pacific Ocean may have seen early Japanese victories but by now was being steadily lost by Japan, a country with no raw materials and overstretched defences.

The apparent ascendancy of totalitarianism was heartening to many in Argentina who believed the defeat of England and the United States could work to the advantage of a country whose dependency on Britain was historic. According to them a totalitarian victory could have made Argentina a key player in South America.

The politics of vote rigging (more blatant after the death of Ortiz and his replacement by the Conservative Castillo) had given democracy a bad name. Defending democracy made no sense to those who could see that elections were rigged. The high-sounding hypocrisy of the country's leaders, who tried to justify these events by calling them minor episodes, had lowered the defences of those who sincerely believed in the democratic system. Nor was there much enthusiasm for defending democracy from the political forces who felt they had a say in defending the democratic system. These forces were trapped between the advance of totalitarian ideas and a few champions of democracy such as Justo, who found himself spearheading support for the Allies in Argentina. And yet Justo himself had been the inventor of vote rigging and scion of the first ban on Radicalism in 1931.

SILENT CHANGE

Elsewhere in the country society had been changing quietly and discreetly. As I have said, economic crisis in 1930 gradually forced many workers from the country to the outskirts of the big cities. In the factories and workshops they sought salaries more suited to their needs, a better standard of living and a social life they did not have in the country. This silent workforce had become part of a limited industrial base, rudimentary but favoured by the crisis, which was making it difficult to import certain goods.

After 1939 the situation became more pronounced: there were so many products that could not be imported from Europe that, however badly, they began to be manufactured in Argentina, and this workforce of country folk benefited from special status, high salaries and full employment, a rare state of affairs for Argentina. They modified the beliefs and expectations of the collective spirit, which were considerably different from those that defined society in the mid-thirties.

Lastly, there existed a nationalist ideology which had no political party to represent it but was prevalent in the military and the upper classes. It expressed a vague need to defend national industry, to depend less on Britain and generally feel more in control of what was ours. In intellectual circles it was also spread by the intense propaganda coming from Spain after Franco's victory. Spain played on its role as mother to Latin America and its historical and emotional ties with countries like Argentina. The idea of Latin America's Hispanic roots was played off against its links with the United States or Britain.

Nationalism was especially important in the Armed Forces, who were pampered under Castillo. They had managed to have a few industrial bodies set up that were dependent on the Army and Navy, whose activities were no longer purely military. The main players in this kind of military-related industrial production were Mosconi and especially Savio. The Armed forces paid close attention to what was happening in Europe. At home, they viewed the politicking of election fraud and hypocrisy with scorn and concocted the idea of a purifying apolitical break with the system. In its place they wanted to establish a superior hierarchy, which would be able to raise Argentina to the status they sought and which the violent corruption of the democratic system could apparently not attain.

So, by mid-1943 there was good reason to believe that something of this nature might happen. But it was a trivial event that finally triggered off the coup. The Radical Party had lost its great leader, Marcelo T. de Alvear, the year before and there was no one who had the charisma to replace him. Justo had died in January 1943 thus throwing the planned democratic front off balance. The Radicals were seeking common ground with the Socialists and Progressive Democrats, a sort of democratic union which would demonstrate to Castillo that not all the civilian population could be deceived.

Castillo used to justify himself by saying that vote rigging had been necessary to stop the Radicals getting their hands on power after their disastrous handling of the country. But his excuses would not hold water against a Radical, Progressive Democrat (still highly respected even after Lisandro de la Torre's death) and Socialist alliance. The alliance moreover had the tacit support of the Communist Party which, though illegal, was still active. These parties held meetings to find a manifesto and a common ticket to fight the forthcoming elections set for September 1943.

In February 1943 Castillo (a pig-headed man) himself named Robustiano Patrón Costa as presidential candidate and, despite the unease it provoked in the Conservative ranks especially in Buenos Aires Province, he was accepted. Patrón Costa was an industrialist from Salta who, curiously enough, sympathised with the Allied cause and not Argentinian neutrality as might have been expected from a man hand-picked by Castillo.

So the electoral battle to be waged panned out like this: on one side, the democratic front, which had not yet chosen a candidate but would be made up of the traditional parties; on the other, the Conservatives and Antipersonalists newly united under the *Concordancia* and brandishing the name of Patrón Costa as their running candidate.

Then, in the middle of everything, a group of Radicals had a brainwave, namely, to hand the presidential candidacy of the Democratic Front to War Minister, General Pedro Pablo Ramírez. They surmised that an active soldier would not let himself be beaten by vote rigging, much less a War Minister; the Radical Party would thus win the elections and once again be in government. They had talks with General Ramírez, who apparently welcomed the idea. Castillo heard about this and called for public clarification. Ramírez issued a rather ambiguous statement and the president ordered him to withdraw his candidacy. Campo de Mayo rose up in arms at this and on 4 June 1943 they deposed the president.

THE *GOU*

From March 1943 a secret lodge of nationalist officers, the *GOU* or *Grupo de Oficiales Unidos* (Group of United Officers) happened to be operating in the Army and it was they who were responsible for starting the military coup without having any real manifesto or leader to speak of. The head of operations was General Rawson. As such he should have become the de facto president but his own companions vetoed him because they did not like some of the names he put forward for ministerial posts. A young colonel called Juan

Perón, who until recently had been in Europe on a study trip, also had a certain standing in the *GOU*.

The result of a trivial event, the coup and resulting government were a fiasco. The Campo de Mayo regiments marched on Government House without a clear agenda under a chief who could not take power. In the end, the deposed president's ex-War Minister, General Ramírez, took charge, a move that smacks of treason and contradiction, and shows that the Army (or rather the Campo de Mayo garrison) had embarked on the coup without really knowing what they were doing. Everybody knew what was not wanted but nobody had a clear idea of what needed to be done.

Thus a de facto government was set up, which from the outset looked very suspect to the Allies, especially to the United States. Precisely because of their lack of an agenda, the coup leaders in '43 handed over certain important posts to some nationalist groups they were having talks with. The nationalists were the only people who at least had a script and could add substance to the revolutionary government, which is just what they did, but in such a way as to incite the condemnation of democratic, intellectual and academic groups. The first steps the de facto government took in this nationalist phase were to impose Catholic religious education on schools, dissolve all political parties and silence many intellectuals who had been calling for Argentina to face up to her international commitments.

It quickly earned the dislike of all the groups who had at first looked on Castillo's defeat with considerable sympathy: he had not been popular, his presidency reeked of illegitimacy and, his undoubted patriotism apart, he increasingly inclined towards the kind of nationalism typical of the de facto government that succeeded him, especially in his obstinate stance over neutrality.

By late 1943, there was no mistaking the outcome of the Second World War and yet the military from Campo de Mayo turned neutrality into a question of principles, an impassioned defence of sovereignty. In January 1944 a tragicomic episode occurred. An Argentinian honorary consul was detained by the allies on a trip around Europe and he was found to have been buying arms in Germany for the Argentinian Army. The United States State Department presented the de facto government with an ultimatum and Ramírez was forced to break off relations with the Axis powers.

This caused such a stir that the Army deposed Ramírez and replaced him with his War Minister, General Farrell. Farrell was not particularly bright but he was more conciliatory and malleable. From then on the de facto government tried to handle international affairs as best it could. The international situation was increasingly adverse and Farrell's government was steadily being isolated by a concerted, United States-inspired, inter-American policy under which all American countries withdrew their ambassadors from Buenos Aires as a criticism of Argentina's neutral posture.

None of this had any direct influence on the economy or our standard of living. The economy was at the peak of prosperity. For one thing, there was an absence of imported goods, which were instead being manufactured locally. Secondly, exportable raw materials from Argentina were well-placed in the European markets, precisely because no lesser person than Winston Churchill objected to the isolation policy being waged by the United States against Argentina. Churchill asked Roosevelt on several occasions not to be too hard on Argentina because Britain needed our meat. He argued that Britain could not be so scrupulous with a neutral country when it respected the neutrality of Ireland.

However that may be, the isolation policy continued without directly affecting Argentina's economy. On the contrary, this was one of its high points: there was a good standard of living, full employment and astronomical earnings from exports, which turned Argentina into Britain's creditor. A few things were lacking of course, such as women's stockings, cosmetics, tyres or fuel, but these were on the whole replaceable things and trains burnt corn cobs instead of coal. A good number of small industries sprang up, potential voters that Perón would later benefit from. He it was, in this political conundrum, who began to justify the provisional government (composed as it was of civilians as far apart as nationalists and Radicals) by emphasising a policy of "social justice".

In March 1945 towards the end of the war in Europe, the Argentinian government was forced to declare war on Germany and

Japan under threat of not being allowed to join the United Nations, a requisite for which was to have declared war on the Axis powers. March 1945 was possibly the nadir of the military government's prestige: they had declared war on two defeated countries; the universities, which ever since have been bastions of anti-government feeling, were returned to normal; and Mr. Spruille Braden, the United States ambassador and the man who was to coordinate the anti-government action, arrived in Buenos Aires.

Braden was an American diplomat who had been to several Latin American countries, Argentina included, and was influential among upper class *Porteños*. He had an obsession that the State Department was quick to endorse. His theory was that the United States had waged an epic struggle against totalitarianism and won, at least in Europe (it was to end the war in Asia by August). But it was absurd in his opinion to leave Fascist foci like Spain and Argentina; governments like these had to be overthrown by lending a helping hand to their opposition parties.

Braden came to Argentina to put together an opposition front that would force the military government to call free elections and hand over power to traditional democratic forces. Throughout 1945 Braden conducted what amounted to an election campaign, during which he travelled to various parts of the country, made speeches that were printed in the major newspapers and brought together all the groups opposed to the military government. He seized the opportunity in September (the government had lifted martial law in August) to take part in the great *Marcha de la Constitución y la Libertad* (March for the Constitution and Freedom), which filled the streets of Buenos Aires to overflowing and called for an end to the de facto government.

PERÓN

But there was one thing the government could salvage: Juan Perón's record at the *Secretaría de Trabajo* (Department of Labour). Perón had taken over in November 1943, a few months after the coup, and used this base to approach the traditional trade unions. He found the *Confederación General del Trabajo* (*CGT*; General Labour Confederation) divided into two camps and allied himself with one of them while simultaneously supplanting the other. He hounded the *CGT*'s socialist or communist leaders and gave non-communists and socialists preferential treatment. He set up new unions and announced new rules for various trades. He put up wages and drew up plans for workers' rights, things like legal redress for wrongful dismissal, paid holidays and a yearly bonus amongst others. But the vital thing Perón did at the Department of Labour was to organise a series of trades with no union tradition.

Many people who had arrived in the city from rural areas were unaware of the concept of unionisation, which was dominated by workers from communist, socialist or anarchist traditions: sugar workers in Tucumán or workers in the big cities where there was no unionisation or where communists and socialists had not been able to unite all the members of a trade, did not know what a trade union was. From the *Secretaría*, Perón drew up rules and regulations for them, organised their meetings, found headquarters for them, worked for their recognition in every way possible and thus created a movement in which previously unfocused loyalties focused on him. He made some clever moves, such as sending the son of a railway worker, Domingo Mercante, to persuade the mainly socialist rail unions to support him.

Pounded by the opposition during 1945, the government sought contact with the Radical Party to negotiate a back door that would allow the military who sided with the government not to be brought to trial. Agreement was sought on the basis of Perón's social policy, the sole justification for what had been accomplished by the de facto government in its two years in office. Nothing came of these negotiations. The Radical leadership held true to Alvear's policies and the hard core *Yrigoyenistas* were not interested in striking an agreement with Perón.

In spite of everything, the government managed to muster three or four Radical leaders as ministers. They took office in August 1945, martial law was lifted and political parties reinstated: this was when the crucial March for the Constitution and Freedom took place and was followed by an attempted military coup in Córdoba that was put down in the nick of time.

OCTOBER 17

Eventually the government reinstated martial law. The situation grew extremely tense. Opposition leaders were arrested en masse and on October 8 a decisive event occurred. The Campo de Mayo garrison called on President Farrell to ask Perón for his resignation. Although it was the same garrison that had been instrumental in the 1943 Revolution and that had been Perón's military backers, it was now under pressure from public opinion, the opposition, the American embassy and the universities. Support for Perón had slumped and he resigned without a fight. Several days of chaos followed, during which the opposition did not manage to fill the vacuum left by Perón. In the meantime, his friends were working in secret to try and get the *CGT* and other unions to rebel.

General Avalos, the commander-in-chief at Campo de Mayo and the brains behind the movement against Perón, offered Sabatini, the governor of Córdoba and leader of the hard core Radicals, the opportunity of having his men in the cabinet, thus creating the conditions for a clear electoral solution which Sabatini himself would benefit from. There were factions within the Radical Party who were opposed to this kind of deal and called for power to be handed over to the Supreme Court of Justice. This was unacceptable to the Army because it was tantamount to admitting their defeat but there was no other flag for such incompatible ideologies as Conservatism, Communism, Radicalism and Socialism to rally round.

October 17 was a truly momentous day. It was a day of public reaction to Perón being held on the island of Martín García (a military camp at the confluence of the Paraná and Uruguay Rivers) and subsequently in the Military Hospital in Buenos Aires; a day on which thousands of workers took to the Plaza de Mayo calling for his freedom. The event, backed up by the Army (or at least by its non-participation), gave rise to a new political regime that held sway for the next ten years: a union movement backing a government supported by the Armed Forces; and the emergence of the non-affiliated masses loyal to a man who fought and won many battles on their behalf. 17 October 1945 marks the end of the old politics and this was to have repercussions at the polls.

Perón asked the Army to pension him off and henceforth devoted all his energies to creating a front of centre-left union leaders. His agenda was very similar to the English Labour Party, who had recently won the first elections after the war and replaced Churchill's Conservatives. Perón sought out Radical leaders with Yrigoyenist leanings with whom he formed the *Unión Cívica Radical-Junta Renovadora* (Radical Civic Union Renovation Committee). Though well out of touch with the contemporary scene, the *Yrigoyenistas* still had political know-how. Colonel Perón Civic Centres also appeared run by Conservatives who had now switched their sympathies to the new leader.

A united front of labour, renovation-minded Radicals and independent civic centres gathered around Perón. He also had considerable invisible support from nationalist groups who were dreaming of a *caudillo* messiah who would open up direct channels of communication between the leadership and the masses. The Church too felt sympathy for this Catholic soldier: Perón had pledged his sword to the Virgin of Luján.

The anti-Peronist opposition consisted of the Radical Party whose candidates, Tamborini and Mosca, the honourable representatives of traditional politics, were openly adopted by the Socialist Party and the Progressive Democratic Party, and on a tacit understanding by the Conservatives. It was a front that could not have existed in 1943 and it now set out to undermine Perón's presidential ambitions.

CAMPAIGN AND ELECTION

It was quite a violent campaign. In December, the government launched the statutory annual bonus, by which workers receive an extra month's salary. This was opposed by businessmen and rejected by the Democratic Union, which, along with the blue book published in Washington in February 1945, would be a determining factor in Perón's close-run victory of 24 February 1946. Perón's subsequent triumph meant new hope for a new Argentina.

Argentina had come out of the war unscathed, was not aligned to the United States and had maintained its dignity and sovereignty. Its products were needed by a starving Europe and new waves of immigrants were coming over to escape the horror and misery of the post-war world. Argentina wanted something the old political parties could no longer give it and the Democratic Union, even in its physical appearance, represented the old, traditional Argentina.

Perón's action might or might not have been a leap into the void but it certainly was new. This was a man who had no political manifesto other than "social action" and whose totalitarian sympathies were rather suspect. But at the same time he introduced a new, unconventional political language, rolled his shirt sleeves up when he spoke in public and was often seen with his wife, a radio actress who was a household name and of whom he was very proud. He tuned into a series of ideas that were in the air at the time: that the State should play a stronger role in the economy; that it should be committed to the underprivileged; the ideas of "social justice" and "sovereignty". He was a man who could quote Pope Leo XIII, Lenin or Yrigoyen and, having only just turned fifty, he had the versatility of youth on his side.

On the other side of the political fence was a corrupt Argentina which, although it had men who had fought long and hard against vote rigging and Fascism, had nevertheless been tainted by the corruption of the old ways. Perón was linked to good times, full employment, high wages, zero inflation and a wealth of social and cultural assets.

The people embraced the new proposition. The elections were very close (52 % against around 47 % for the Democratic Union) but the Sáenz Peña Law allowed Perón to carry off 13 of the 14 provinces (the only province with an opposition government was Corrientes), two thirds of the Chamber of Deputies and almost the whole of the Senate.

One might say that the almost absurd coup of 1943 was justified by Perón's election victory of 4 June 1946. Indeed, this was the only de facto process in Argentina that has had any success at the polls. All the rest have failed miserably.

CHAPTER XII
THE HEYDAY OF PERONISM

Although a host of books, articles, monographs and research papers have been written in both Argentina and abroad trying to explain what Peronism was, in my opinion none has managed to come up with a true definition of this curious and most Argentinian of phenomena. Some speak of populism or backwardness; others of soft Fascism or of a peculiarly Latin America system in which the army has a single-party hegemony. But these definitions, though useful for political scientists, are of no great matter to us. We must now get down to hard facts, to try in some way to tackle this early Peronist experiment unparalleled in Argentinian history. Therefore in this chapter we shall put theory on one side.

Juan Domingo Perón was president from 4 June 1946 to the same date of 1952. On 4 June 1952 he took office for a second time by virtue of the constitutional reform of 1949 but did not see out his term because of the military coup of September 1955.

These two terms of office, though broadly similar, were in some details quite different. In this chapter we shall concentrate on Perón's first term from various different angles, since a total appreciation of the period is well nigh impossible. We shall begin by looking at aspects of the economy (perhaps the new government's most original undertaking), then at politics, the opposition, the world at large and the conspicuous presence of Perón's wife, Evita.

THE ECONOMY

The Peronist economy was in its early stages nationalistic, statist and autarkist. It was nationalistic in that there was a drive to 'nationalise'; in other words, to transfer a whole series of activities and services that had until then been in the hands of foreign countries or companies to Argentina herself, for example, the repatriation of the foreign debt. On coming to power Perón repatriated the country's fairly insignificant foreign debt. He bought back securities from abroad on which minimal interest was accruing in order to turn the foreign debt into a domestic one. There was bitter criticism from some quarters claiming that the sums being paid out to foreign creditors in debt repayments and interest were tiny, whereas the sums needed to acquire the debt were excessively large.

One must remember that during the Second World War Argentina had accumulated considerable reserves in Britain which, for the first time in its history, had made it a creditor nation. It was reinforced by its position as a supplier of raw materials (above all cereals and oil-based products) in a world that was only just beginning to rebuild its systems of production after the war. Perón and his economic policy were to an extent the expression of the Argentina I described in the previous chapter: triumphant and unscathed, and with a sense of its own importance on the world stage. Its produce was crucial for Europe and it was the darling of the United States, despite the latter's earlier differences with the de facto governments.

The statism of Perón's first presidency was due to the powerful influence the government had acquired in economic matters. Even given Conservative interventionism in the thirties, it had so far played a relatively secondary role. The State did not have control over any of the major public service sectors other than a small fraction of the railways.

To cut a long story short, the State came to control all rail transport after 1946 via its purchase of the English-owned railways (completed by 1948 and preceded by the purchase of the less substantial French-owned railways). It also controlled the nationwide gas supply after it purchased the originally British *Compañía Primitiva de Gas*, (First Gas Company) and the national grid after acquiring power stations in the provinces. In Buenos Aires and Greater Buenos Aires, however, the distribution of power continued to be run by the CHADE, the international holding company that had been at the forefront of a scandal in the thirties and that, mysteriously enough, Perón treated with the utmost respect. This becomes less mysterious when we learn that the CHADE's directors put up money for Perón's election campaign and that Perón repaid the compliment by letting the CHADE continue running the service in the Federal Capital (although without renewing its utilities, a fact that would later cause serious problems).

The State also controlled a long list of other operations, including river transport after purchasing the Compañía Dodero, domestic and foreign flights after the creation of four companies that later merged to create Aerolíneas Argentinas, and foreign trade in oil-based products, cereals and other important exports. The State would buy produce from the farmer at a given price, effectively taking over what companies like Bunge y Born or Dreyfus had been doing for many years, and then sell it abroad, usually making a significant profit in the process. Such transactions were performed by the *Instituto Argentino de Promoción de Intercambio* (*IAPI*; Argentine Institute for the Promotion of Exchange), through which the State imported the goods (manufactured or otherwise) that the country was thought to need to keep the whole cycle going. The process was not always carried out as it should have been and large quantities of material often ended up rotting in warehouses in Customs.

Influence over public and foreign services came from the State's say in credit, economic and monetary policy, and was implemented through the nationalisation of the Central Bank. The Central Bank, created under the Conservatives in the thirties, had a board of directors made up of representatives from both public and private banks. Before taking over the Presidency in June 1946 Perón had called on the de facto government to nationalise the Central Bank by returning the private banks' original contributions, which effectively made the Central Bank the sole representative of official banking practice.

In addition to this, Peronist monetary policy ingeniously involved the State guaranteeing all bank deposits and confiscating all the money in the country in return. This was all on paper of course but, as a consideration for the guarantee, the Central Bank was to fix the guidelines for all the banks (state and private) for credit and rediscount policies. So, from then on Argentina's credit and monetary policy was firmly in the hands of a government-controlled Central Bank.

State activities not related to the public service sector involved German companies confiscated after the declaration of war in March 1945. This meant that the State was ultimately the owner of several companies manufacturing anything from medicinal products to cosmetics.

In short the State had great influence on the country's economy. The number of civil servants went up considerably and the amount of red-tape began to get worse when Perón's economic policy ran into a few hitches. The government undertook various drives to lower the cost of living, regulate prices, subsidise bakeries or meat processing plants, or as a penalty against any "unscrupulous" traders who were pushing their prices up. The State then was such a powerful force in the economy that it is no exaggeration to label Perón's policies out-and-out statism.

The autarkist nature of the economy was basically due to the idea that Argentina had sufficient capacity and such varied production as to be potentially almost totally self-sufficient. The protection of industry through customs barriers, along with the *IAPI* policy of purchasing agricultural produce for subsequent sale abroad, meant an enormous shift of resources from the rural to the industrial sector.

This all had a logical explanation, namely, the advantageous position Argentina found itself in after the Second World War. But there was a drawback: the fact that at some stage it had to come to an end. The international economy quickly began to grow stronger and the Bretton Woods accords, which attempted to liberalise international trade and opposed various countries' restrictive subsidy policies, began to be implemented. Under the circumstances, Argentina (which was no longer a creditor nation since it had been spending its accumulated reserves by buying up the railways, repatriating its foreign debt and acquiring the capital assets of foreign companies who had set up business here) found its policies more and more difficult to uphold. The days of interventionism, statism, autarkism and nationalism were numbered unless two of Perón's predictions came true. Neither did.

NEW DIRECTIONS

The first of Perón's wagers was that a third world war would break out. He was convinced that the United States and the Soviet Union would at any moment lock horns, a conflict that would benefit Argentina just as the first and second world wars had. Even though a third world war never came, Perón's bet was not that far wide of the mark. In 1950 the Korean War broke out. Its real antagonists were the USA and the USSR and it could easily have escalated to reach uncontrollable proportions. However, in the end it was waged on Korean territory and did not ignite the world war Perón was forecasting in his articles in *Democracia* under the transparent pen-name of Descartes.

His other wager had less tangible evidence behind it. He predicted the rise of an Argentinian bourgeoisie with sufficient economic resources to create new sources of labour and establish an industry that had no need of heavy subsidies or protection. Perón reckoned that, if the State allied itself with this bourgeoisie, together they could kickstart the economy and usher in a new age of prosperity. The problem was that either this bourgeoisie did not exist, or it was too easily scared and did not have adequate guarantees for it to be able to invest its surpluses in non-traditional activities.

So much so that the ebullience which in 1946 had brought Perón to boast that you couldn't walk through the Central Bank for the gold stacked up in it, had by 1951 or 1952 turned into anxiety. The Argentine peso, which in 1946 was backed 130 percent by foreign currency and gold, had by 1952 fallen to 15 percent. Argentina's foreign currency had evaporated; our gold and dollar reserves from the war had vanished into thin air. The need for a new direction was answered after Perón had been elected for a second term in 1951.

Perón's bold, high-risk economic policy was to a great extent the brain-child of Miguel Miranda, a tinplate industrialist with a highly original personality. He was an economist with a talent for virtuoso improvisation, which Argentina had to pay for as dearly as it reaped the benefits from his strokes of genius.

As president of the Central Bank, Miranda was the tsar of the economy. Although Argentina had a Treasury, a Trade Department and such like, he was the man who really pulled the strings of the economy. This state of affairs lasted until January 1949, when Miranda was forced to resign and Perón initiated a gradualist change in economic policy. The economy was no longer to be led by one powerful politician but by a cast of bureaucrats among whom Alfredo Gómez Morales distinguished himself early on and later the young Antonio Cafiero.

Perón's policy, which to us looks pretty reckless, did have an explanation: quite apart from Argentina's strong post-war standing, much of the major countries' thinking at the time coincided with the idea of an economically influential State aiming at a more even distribution of wealth; at nationalising the public service sector, banks and major industries (as indeed occurred in England after the 1945 Labour victory, or in France after the Liberation, when De Gaulle nationalised several major companies including car manufacturers). In other words, statism was the order of the day.

A wing of the Radical Party, responding to the Intransigence Movement, which took over the party after 1948, thought along the same lines. The Avellaneda Declaration (signed in 1945, extended in 1946 and becoming party policy as from 1948) also advanced nationalistic, autarkist and statist ideas along the same lines as those Perón had adopted. However, such measures, which may have been necessary at one time, would after a while begin to come apart at the seams. Perón did not take this eventuality into account, or noticed it only when the relevant adjustments entailed too high a price to pay.

Anyway around 1951 or 1952 the government's economic policy was beginning to wear thin, (which does not mean that people had noticed). Generally speaking, people were living happier, fuller lives. Their money went further than it used to: by 1950 an average blue-collar building worker was earning twenty percent more than in 1943 and was exercising his new spending power mainly on clothing, food and fun.

After this policy had been running for a little while, the standard of living also deteriorated because it was getting more difficult to shore up an economy that badly needed dollars to stay afloat. There was need for fuel, for example and *YPF*, the state-owned oil company, had not increased production over this period; neither had the private oil companies. As a result desperately needed fuel was costing the country 300 million dollars, which in those days was a lot of money that Argentina no longer had at its disposal. The outlay needed to keep a largely subsidised and protected industry afloat was considerable and money was also needed to pay royalties or the remittance on profits of foreign firms based in Argentina.

This was very difficult to maintain with a policy like Perón's. The swingeing droughts of 1950 and 1951, which undermined the country's grain exports and the reluctance of rural producers taxed to the hilt did not help. When European prices were high and our exports were required, the *IAPI* would act as a third party on behalf of the State by buying up rural produce and selling it abroad at a fabulous profit. The very lack of foreign currency made rural mechanisation extremely difficult and brought production to a virtual standstill. By 1951 and 1952 the area of crops sown in Argentina had fallen catastrophically. Yet, the significance of all this only began to be noticed after Perón's re-election in 1952.

POLITICAL ANGLES

Peronism was also a political one-off: it was clearly authoritarian, populist and tended towards a single party system. The Peronist Movement consisted of the *Partido Peronista Masculino* (Men's Peronist Party) and, when after 1949 women were given the vote, the *Partido Peronista Femenino* (Women's Peronist Party), the third element being the *CGT*.

From the outset, even before Perón took over the government, he was anxious to organise the political instruments he would have to possess in order to wield power. Thus, before legally taking office in 1946, he decided to dissolve the political forces that had voted for him the previous February. Out of the remnants he founded a single party, which at first had no name, but was later called the *Partido*

Único de la Revolución Nacional (Sole Party of National Revolution) and eventually came to be known as the Peronist Party.

The Peronist Party therefore became the government's political mouthpiece. It was made up of believers and enthusiasts but also of a kind of closed shop of state employees. It was a party that enjoyed conspicuous official patronage that manifested itself in various ways. The most striking of these was the way the government together with the Party's third branch, the *CGT*, which in 1950 had declared itself an official part of *Justicialismo*, took a leading role in the management of the State.

This should be viewed as part of the Peronist government's authoritarianism, which from the first took a hostile attitude towards its opponents. In the previous chapter we mentioned that, despite its narrow majority in the 1946 elections, the electoral system gave Perón the virtually unanimous support of the Senate, two thirds of the Chamber of Deputies and all the provincial governments except Corrientes, which was brought into line a year later. In other words he had the undivided consensus of Argentina.

But as if that was not enough, Perón went and bought up all the private radio stations in the country, set up a chain of government newspapers and magazines and applied constant pressure to the opposition, who as I have said had scant parliamentary representation and therefore were virtually powerless to oppose Perón's policies. Yet the way in which the opposition was treated suggested that Perón believed they were constantly plotting to overthrow him.

A "movement" like Peronism was disastrous for Argentinian politics because a priori it established the idea that Peronism embodied the nation's will, the will of the people, of history itself. Anyone who stood against Perón was in effect a traitor. The treatment dished out to the opposition was very harsh. Radical deputies were often prevented from speaking in Congress; some were expelled and others, like Ricardo Balbín, were imprisoned or driven into exile.

Political parties led an active but high-pressure life, a life full of persecution and danger. Election campaigns were not easy. There was no access to the radio stations. There were only two independent national newspapers of any standing, *La Nación* and *La Prensa*. The latter was effectively silenced in 1951 when it was closed down on a fine point of union policy and eventually seized by the government only to be handed over to the *CGT*. Peronist propaganda and publicity were handled by a slick State organisation that would not allow any comment disagreeable to the government to filter through.

This was a climate in which the opposition was treated as if it were a black cloud hanging over the country; a sector which had to be ostracised from the political process for not sharing the ideals of the majority. Nothing remotely like tolerance or pluralism existed during Perón's years as president. On the contrary, a hostile attitude prevailed fostered by Perón himself. In many of his speeches he had harsh even deranged words for the opposition parties: he threatened to hang them and with his own baling wire if they vexed a government that had the support of the people. In such a harsh climate the opposition had no loyalty to the government. Wild plots to overthrow Perón abounded, almost none of which had any chance of success.

Who was at fault? I personally believe that in these cases it is governments who must bear the brunt of the blame. They should in general be endowed with more patience and tolerance than the opposition and Perón was anything but a model of patience and tolerance. But at this point we should put a name to the figure who played such a significant part in arousing the kind of fanaticism surrounding Perón: Eva Duarte de Perón.

EVITA

It is unfair to have spent so little time analysing the impact of Perón's wife, Evita, on the political scene, given the curiosity she has aroused in observers both in Argentina and abroad. Nevertheless, her presence in the Peronist government might be said to have served several functions: firstly, to establish contact between the government and the workers' movement through the unions; secondly, as the natural leader of the Women's Peronist Party, a new body of voters of immense logistical importance; and lastly, Evita's ragged fanatical oratory, which inspired in the Peronist ranks a kind of mysticism. Six years is a very long time indeed to keep up a mystique yet Evita did so until her health gave out.

These three functions, together with running a kind of informal Ministry of Social Welfare from the Foundation which bore her name, gave Evita extraordinary charisma. For an uneducated woman she had acute intuition, knew how to handle herself in public and was a skilled propagandist. In the last years of her life she began to get more militant and could even look the part.

I for one respect Evita as a very genuine woman. But I would not like to see the likes of her again in our country. In every possible way she signified a backward step in the political life of Argentina. She gave us tremendous fanaticism, demanded unconditional adherence to the Peronist cause and this did the republican system nothing but harm. She died very shortly after Perón became president for the second time.

THE 1949 CONSTITUTION

The other aspect to be born in mind when looking at early Peronist politics is the 1949 Constitution. Regardless of his inaugural speech in which he claimed he would be president for all Argentinians, promising tolerance and understanding for those who did not think his way, Perón began to sketch the outlines of an authoritarian hegemony from the very moment he took office. Perón's first concern was to set up a power structure that would let him realise his goals and then take his time in catching the public's eye. With this in mind, he attempted to get rid of any institutional obstacles in his path.

His first hurdle was the Supreme Court. In 1948 he put all the judges in the Supreme Court except one on trial and dismissed them on grounds of malpractice. They were not convicted of anything specific. The charges brought against them were a political attempt to replace the Court with another that would not cause any trouble.

This was the first time in Argentinian politics that anything like this had happened and, let us hope, it will be the last. Apart from anything, the episode was extremely unfair and insulted the values of the judicial system. But to Perón and his associates it must have seemed essential not to have any obstacles in the way of future legislation. This in itself was not so revolutionary that it would have been rejected by the original Supreme Court, which consisted of old Conservatives who had proved themselves malleable enough in the past.

Thereafter Perón's re-election became a kind of dash for the finishing post. The 1853 Constitution barred a president's immediate re-election and so a programme of reforms was launched. The strange thing is that in one paragraph of the 1948 Legislative Assembly's inauguration speech Perón lays out the best possible arguments against presidential re-election. And very sensible, familiar arguments they were too: in some sense re-election was a chance to achieve permanent arbitrariness, the perpetuation of one man's power.

Nevertheless, a few months later Perón accepted the idea of reforming the Constitution, which was incorrectly voted on by the Chamber of Deputies: their majority was unconstitutional and the clauses to be reformed in the text were never stipulated in accordance with constitutional practice. But anyway the mechanism of reform got under way, elections were called and as usual the Peronist Party won a landslide victory. The Constituent Convention finally took place between January and April of 1949.

Despite rhetorical additions, the basis of the 1853 Constitution remained untouched. The key addition however was the new possibility of re-electing presidents indefinitely. This became transparently clear when in one decisive session Moisés Lebensohn, the president of the Radical bloc, hounded a member of the majority party into confessing that the whole reform was in fact nothing but a pretext to re-elect Perón.

The 1949 Constitution established a new power structure and the prospect that Perón would be re-elected in 1952 for another six years; in other words, his presidency would last at least twelve years and might be extended ad infinitum. But it also established several clauses beyond Perón's control: Article 40 stipulated a series of highly inflexible guidelines regarding the public service sector, ownership of mineral deposits, waterfalls and hydroelectric power sources. Such clauses were to dog Perón's future reforms to his economic policy.

As we saw earlier, Miranda had resigned in January 1949, when the Convention began sitting, an omen of economic reform. A small group of conventional nationalistic Peronists managed to introduce Article 40 and thus restrict Perón's economic options, a fact that would in 1955 be of extreme importance.

THE INTERNATIONAL SCENE

Peronism, for all its political and economic peculiarities, was acted out in the context of a cold war that was getting ever icier. The United States was looking for allies and Argentina was potentially a good friend to have. However, in 1949 Perón launched his so-called "Third Position": he announced to the world that Argentina was neither pro-Soviet Union nor pro-United States, but maintained a different stance. The Third Position was a foretaste of what would later become the Non-Aligned Movement, which our country has recently left following the decision, paradoxically enough, of a Peronist government.

But this stance was more of a rhetorical gesture than anything else. In major international forums such as the United Nations, Argentinian delegations have almost always voted together with the United States. But the Third Position did not support the IMF or UNESCO or the FAO and this kept the country in a state of isolation that was basically in line with autarkic Peronist economic policy.

Be that as it may, the Third Position for all its rhetoric imbued the Argentinian populace with a feeling of nationalism and gave them a sense that Argentina could rise above the vagaries of international politics, even though this stance was ultimately no different from Yrigoyen's neutrality during the First World War or Castillo's and the de facto military government's during the Second.

The idea behind the Third Position was the prospect of a third world war which, though it never happened, nevertheless gave Perón the opportunity to make certain gestures, especially where his relationship with the United States was concerned. This task he accomplished with some skill and by around 1953 Argentina's relationship with the States began to develop towards total agreement. In addition to all this however, we should analyse the opposition's stance during the six years of Perón's first term as president.

THE OPPOSITION

Perón was opposed by the traditional political parties, who had been well and truly beaten in the 1946 elections. The only party to come out of these elections with anything like enough support to lead the opposition to Perón was the Radical Party. With 44 deputies in Congress they formed a closely allied front made up of figures such as Arturo Frondizi, Ricardo Balbín and others, who would in many cases go on to have long political careers. Some of them put up a respectable, well-thought-out opposition, while others, understandably, allowed themselves to be thrown off balance by Perón's disorienting tactics, and their opposition descended into a simple struggle for survival.

But the fringes of the bloc, more in the intransigent, non-unionist tradition of Yrigoyen than of Alvear, gradually began to rebuild Radicalism. In 1948, as I have already mentioned, this movement won the party leadership and turned the ideals and policies of the Intransigent Movement (as statist and neutralist as Perón's and more anti-oligarchic and anti-imperialist, one might even say more revolutionary) into party policy. Moreover, this thinking was encouraged by a party that, with no chance of gaining power, could so to speak play with ideas with impunity.

Compared to the Radicals, the Conservatives were effectively all washed up and had very few votes in the elections. The Socialists had not a single representative in the Chamber of Deputies for the first time since the Sáenz Peña Law, while the Communists remained underground. But all this does not mean that opposition to Perón only took the form of political parties such as the Radicals or Socialists.

There was also a loosely-knit opposition organised along class lines. Argentina's upper classes were upset at Perón's often crassly aggressive egalitarian tendencies. The fact that anybody who felt like it could suddenly go to the summer resorts that had previously been the domain of an elite outraged many people. Some gentrified institutions out in the country such as the Jockey Club or the Club 20 de Febrero in Salta, were focal points for the opposition and were hounded by the Peronists: the Jockey Club was burnt to the ground and the 20 de Febrero seized, a fate shared by a few other traditional institutions.

In parts of the business world there was muted opposition to Perón. Although this did not make itself felt openly, it did nevertheless exist especially in rural areas, which were the most heavily taxed under Peronist economic policy.

Institutionalised opposition, however, came from the Radical Party. Despite facing enormous difficulties in getting their message across and maintaining their nationwide network, they nevertheless put up a brave fight: in 1951 the Balbín-Frondizi ticket took 32 percent of the vote. Perón took more than 62 percent of the votes, true. But if one thinks of the conditions under which election campaigns were fought at the time, the Radicals' 32 percent was in fact quite an achievement.

Opposition also existed in the Armed Forces. There were groups who did not support or simply disowned Perón, despite the fact that, taking advantage of the country's economic situation, he (himself a general) pushed through the modernisation of the Armed Forces especially his beloved Air Force. Still, there were many reasons for resentment within the Army since chiefs-of-staff and officers who supported the Peronist regime were favoured over and above those who did not.

Although of course this was not the only reason for Menéndez's uprising of 1951, it does go some way to explaining the background to the military coup, which with hindsight had not the slightest chance of succeeding. It was carried out in September 1951 barely two months before the presidential elections and had no repercussions anywhere else in the country. A handful of retired and active officers (among them Captain Lanusse) managed to whip up some disjointed support in Campo de Mayo and then scattered when they realised things were hopeless. Still, this 'revolution' does demonstrate that within the army there were certain hubs of opposition. After the attempted coup of course the War Minister set about cleaning out any anti-Peronists in the Armed Forces.

Perón's first presidency had the appeal of being brand new: Perón at fifty was still young and spoke a language that soon won the people's hearts and allowed him, both nationally and internationally, to advocate a social policy that raised the general standard of living. After Evita's death in 1952, the shortcomings of Perón's economic miracle began to be noticed. When he took office for the second time he was beset by problems like inflation and a shortage of foreign currency, which forced him to make a complete U-turn.

CHAPTER XIII THE COLLAPSE OF THE PERONIST REGIME

Juan Domingo Perón's second government began on 4 June 1952 and should have lasted until the same date in 1958. However, its abrupt interruption in September 1955 raises one of the most burning questions about the period: why did Perón go under?

THE ORGANISED COMMUNITY

Perón's fall from grace was not for lack of power. By the time his system began to founder, he had managed to set up what he called the *Comunidad Organizada* or Organised Community. This consisted of the *CGT*, the *CGE* or General Economic Confederation, the *CGU* or General University Confederation, the Armed Forces, the security forces, education, sports and last but not least a chain of newspapers and magazines which, together with the radio stations, made for an almost unassailable propaganda force.

The Peronist regime moreover had the staunch support of the masses. This made itself felt in 1951, when Perón was elected with more than 60 percent of the vote, and was repeated in the vice-presidential elections of April 1954 with 62 percent in favour of Perón and 32 percent for his nearest opponent, the Radical, Crisólogo Larralde.

All the significant areas of Argentinian life were in one way or another organised by the Justicialist State and mass support not only revealed itself at election time but was clearly visible in the crowds that turned out for the regime's almost liturgical rallies on May 1, October 17 and even on new dates such as August 31, the *Día del Renunciamiento* or "Day of the Renunciation" in honour of Evita, who had died a month and a half after her husband took office for a second time.

So how come he went under? Had his economic policy reached breaking point or something? Not at all. By the time the Peronist regime was in decline its economic policy had been straightened out and some of its earlier bolder initiatives shelved. As I have said, this early stage, a time of euphoric dissipation, had seen some interesting but short-lived initiatives.

When, after 1950, this policy reached its lowest ebb and it became clear that a statist, nationalistic and autarkist approach could not be continued since it entailed an almost total lack of foreign currency and the consequent difficulty of importing certain goods essential to Argentina's livelihood; and when, in 1951, all this translated into inflation figures that reached an unheard-of 30 percent, the government finally changed its tack.

ECONOMIC ADJUSTMENTS

After 1951 and Perón's resounding election victory in November, measures came into effect in February of the following year which amounted to an austerity plan or, as we would now call it, an adjustment plan. The plan evinced the need to cap certain kinds of expenditure and above all to inject new life into agriculture and cattle-raising. These had come to an almost total standstill under the policies of the *IAPI*, which acted as the customary buyer, seller and middleman of staples from the farming world destined for European markets.

Perón made some brutal adjustments to the *IAPI*'s policy by fixing lucrative prices for producers and establishing controls on prices, wages and collective agreements (which were frozen for two years starting in 1952). He thus managed to reduce the annual rate of inflation quite significantly from 4% in 1952 to 3% in 1953. So it was not economic policy that hastened the regime's decline.

Apart from this, from 1952 there were a series of initiatives in the economic order which show that Perón had abandoned high-risk policies for what might be termed classical economics. In January 1949 the mastermind of early Peronist economic policy, Miguel Miranda, had been removed and replaced by less spectacular but more expert teams with an orthodox conception of economics. The passing of measures such as the foreign investment law signified a real step backwards.

Until then Peronism had not shown any great interest in investments from abroad. On the contrary it had looked with a certain disdain on the assumption that the bourgeoisie had sufficient capital to set new enterprises in motion and create new sources of employment. But this did not transpire and in 1951 the law of foreign investments was passed. This might be said to have been a good, moderate law, which recognised the right of foreign capital to send remittances to its country of origin. Foreign investors were given certain guarantees and were brought into the legal framework in which Argentinian companies operated. If nothing else, this move recognised the need for new sources of employment-creating capital.

The apparently unofficial Productivity Conference of April 1955 also showed that economic policy had shifted substantially. This Conference, which was held in the Congress Building, was led by the *CGE* and the *CGT*. In theory the State was not involved. However, in practice it was the government that was encouraging dialogue between the two forces representing business and labour.

From this dialogue the need arose to up productivity even at the expense of the new achievements in work regulations and procedures. Whenever it comes to discussing productivity (anywhere, at any time) trade unions begin to get edgy and the case of Argentina was no different. There was even resistance from some union organisations whose rank and file were not strictly dependent on the official party, despite formal Peronist attachments. But regardless, the Productivity Conference recommended dispensing with certain methods such as the so-called "*industria del despido*" or "redundancy industry", which had become an outrage early on in the regime, as had overtime.

Lastly, the other feature that shows how far Peronism shifted its economic stance during 1954 and especially after 1955 was the negotiation of a contract with American oil company, California. The government was prepared to hand over almost the whole of Santa Cruz Province so that California could drill for oil and set up installations there. One of the grimmest problems Perón had to face as a result of his earlier economic policy was the shortage of fuel and the high price of importing it: the liquid fuel imports needed to keep Argentina's industry working cost 300 million dollars, an expense that was increasingly difficult to meet.

Perón's decision to strike a deal with California was evidence of how far the system found itself with its back against the wall and how far its economic policy had failed in certain respects. The concession went against all the nationalist policies Perón had been preaching and he had to pay for it politically. All the nationalist groups who had been supporting Perón automatically bristled with indignation, while the opposition began to denounce what was seemingly a grave failure on the government's part to practise what it preached. After an initial policy based on the need for a *YPF* monopoly, the government had given away half a national territory for exploitation by an American company.

BIDDING THE THIRD POSITION FAREWELL

Several other things aside from economic policy had changed, for example, the government's stance vis-à-vis the United States. Early on in his first term in 1946, the aftermath of the showdown between Ambassador Braden and Perón was still being felt but later relations were gradually patched up. The Guatemala issue in 1953 revealed how far Perón would go to align himself with the United States on matters of international politics.

Since 1950 Guatemala had had a government with socialist tendencies, which naturally was condemned by Washington as being infiltrated by communists. Determined to apply its social policy, the Guatemalan government had implemented agricultural reforms and confiscated property from the American company United Fruit, which had interests in other countries in Central America. The ensuing condemnation from the Americans was thunderous, so much so that the United States called a conference of Foreign Secretaries in Caracas aiming at denouncing the Guatemalan regime as communist infiltrators of the Pan-American community thus foreshadowing what would happen later in Cuba.

When the Argentinian delegation had to vote all it did was abstain. (Of course, a few years earlier their attitude in a similar situation had been quite different.) To add insult to injury, when a group from within Guatemala overthrew Jacobo Arbenz's regime with American help and some of his officials had to go into hiding in the Argentinian embassy until they were eventually given a plane to take them to Buenos Aires, the Peronist government promptly clapped them in Villa Devoto prison. In other words, the Guatemalan officials who, whether they were communists or not, had believed they could distribute their county's wealth better, came up against Perón who, having been a trailblazer of such politics in Latin America, a touchstone for those who wanted slightly fairer distribution, promptly locked them away for more than a year.

These important changes were not due simply to Perón's wishes but also to force of circumstance. They had begun during 1952 and became more pronounced when in 1953 Perón tried out the most spectacular measure of his policy, namely, to open up Latin American markets. He travelled to Chile to try and persuade General Ibañez's government to sign an agreement that was tantamount to almost total economic union with Argentina. The Chileans resisted and the pact that was eventually signed was much less significant. Still, Perón did score a major political victory in Chile, where he was repeatedly cheered by the crowds.

TOUGHENING UP

On returning to Argentina from Chile in April 1953 he met with an unpleasant surprise. An unexpected conflict over meat supplies in Buenos Aires seemed to suggest the existence of a chain of privileged interests that was working to the detriment of consumers. Perón had the matter investigated by General León Bengoa, a highly principled and enterprising soldier who was convinced he would find no less a man than Perón's private secretary and brother to the late Evita, Juan Duarte, behind these speculative manoeuvres.

True or not, the fact is that Perón gave an extremely inflamed speech (the one where he claims to be "surrounded by thieves and tell-tales" and insists on pursuing the inquiry even if it implicates his own father). The day after came the news of Juan Duarte's resignation and his suicide three days after that sent shockwaves through the country. It was one of the few events the regime's party machine could not cover up. That the president's private secretary and brother-in-law should shoot himself, leaving behind a childishly written letter evincing intense personal distress, was something that tarnished the reputation of the highest echelons of the regime.

In light of this, the *CGT* organised a demonstration in the Plaza de Mayo in support of the president and while Perón was speaking some bombs went off at the entrance to the underground in the Calle Hipólito Yrigoyen killing two or three people and wounding several more. As a result of this and a few carelessly chosen words by Perón when he realised the explosions were bombs, various groups (spontaneously or otherwise) tried setting fire to the Casa del Pueblo (headquarters of the Socialist Party), the Casa Radical (headquarters of the *UCR*), the prestigious Jockey Club, the local headquarters of the Conservative Party, the Petit Café and other dens of opposition iniquity. Members of the opposition were rounded up and several thousand political bigwigs sent to Villa Devoto or the National Penitentiary.

All of a sudden there was a queer tension in the air and things carried on like this for a couple of months until the culprits were found (or so the public were officially informed). They turned out to be a group of youngsters from upper-crust families who occasionally planted bombs. They tried to avoid any casualties while demonstrating a focus of opposition to Perón at a time when there was no form of organisation that could oppose the regime.

The bombs, fires and arrests were terrible but did follow a certain logic. What however does not seem so logical is that two months later Perón proposed a peace initiative to conciliate opposition forces. Talks were held with opposition leaders, some of those under arrest were released and finally in December an arbitrary amnesty was granted to people the Executive deemed eligible. This meant that several dozen political leaders left prison while others like Cipriano Reyes, who had been there since 1948, or the leaders of General Menéndez's uprising of September 1951, or a handful of conspirators led by Colonel José Francisco Suárez, remained inside. Still, it was significant that Perón acknowledged that not all opposition members were traitors, conspirators or terrorists.

Thus 1953 ended on a note of reconciliation. Although the amnesty was of no great significance, it did bring a little peace and tolerance to national politics. This was when the Peronist Party easily won the April 1954 elections with 62 percent of the vote. However in May 1954 a rash of strikes broke out which the propaganda machine covered up. For today's researchers it is a real ordeal to determine the strikes that took place or how extensive they were because there was absolutely no coverage in the newspapers of the day. Any details have to be deduced from provincial newspapers or resistance bulletins. Yet some of these strikes were very stormy indeed. At least one person died in the strike by metalworkers when they marched on the Federal Capital.

Nevertheless, by mid-1954 things were looking up for Perón. He had put an end to the inflation of 1951 and 1952 and prices and wages were relatively stable. There was now talk of foreign investment (born out by the arrival of car plants in Córdoba and metalworking factories in the outskirts of Buenos Aires) and of oil companies being installed in the south.

Politically speaking the coast was clear. The opposition had been crushed. The Radical presence in Congress was minimal, only twelve deputies out of over 200. This was due to a crafty election law that allowed Peronism to take thirteen seats with only 650,000 votes while the Radicals took only one with 500,000 votes.

There were no major problems for Perón on the horizon. His party had accepted the economic adjustments. Some of his more radical collaborators had been ditched. He had by now given up the idea of a third world war and his new friendship with the United States instead promised a good deal. All in all the future could be viewed with a good deal of optimism and Perón was nothing if not an optimist.

CLASHES WITH THE CHURCH

Then suddenly at the end of 1954 (in November to be exact) Perón did something whose political logic is absolutely incomprehensible and less than a year later he was out. I am referring to the speech he gave to governors in the provinces and leaders of his own party, including trade union and women leaders, in which he condemned part of the Catholic Church in Argentina as being the most significant enemy of the day.

It is difficult to see why he did this. Personally, I think the problem was an overweening sense of his own omnipotence. Perón had everything. He pulled the strings of labour, business, journalism, the armed forces and education. There had to be something somewhere that did not fit in with his policies and that something was the Church. By its very nature it could not commit itself to any given policy, even though many of its members were grateful to Perón for compulsory religious education in schools and the general goodwill he had shown Catholicism. But Perón's vulgarly naming the priests and bishops who in his own words were *contreras* (literally 'againsters') could only provoke a reaction from the Church, which at all events acted very sensibly and limited itself to distancing from Perón.

The latter, however, suddenly found himself embroiled in a process he was unable to contain. Some of the men accompanying him, especially those of second or third rank, were at one time or another from the left and the anticlerical tone with which Perón began to spike his rhetoric took them back to the battles of their younger days. The newspapers that were part of the Peronist propaganda machine pounced with equally violent rhetoric. There were sections (not without wit I might add) written by men like Jorge Abelardo Ramos, otherwise known as the *obispero revuelto* (or bishop scruffer, to coin a phrase) which contained the most sordid gossip about the clergy. This kind of thing was printed day in day out to drive the message home to the public.

The Catholic Church slowly began to react. Instead of its usual processional stroll on December 8 to celebrate the Immaculate Conception, the Church held a massive demonstration. It gradually became a united bastion for a previously divided opposition.

The Peronist government intensified its offensive and towards the end of December 1954 Congress passed laws revoking compulsory religious education, authorising brothels to be opened, withdrawing financial support from private (in the main Catholic) educational institutions and permitting divorce, in other words, all the measures that would most annoy the Church. Perón effectively sacrificed the support of various Peronist legislators, above all women. Some, though not very many it must be said, resigned. Still, there were many genuinely Catholic legislators who, though they opted to obey orders from above, were inwardly torn.

The conflict continued. As tends to happen in Argentina, it cooled off in the summer but after April came back to life with a vengeance. In June, after a steady stream of other anticlerical laws, the procession of Corpus Christi took place. Despite being banned, a huge crowd paraded from the Plaza de Mayo to the Congress building. Here Perón, who through all of this had acted as arbitrator, made another typical but no less bewildering blunder. So far he had not been leading hostilities against the Church, though he clearly agreed with the measures that were upsetting it. On occasion he would seem ready to compromise but then suddenly take some action that brought the situation back to boiling point. And naturally church groups, especially the lay Catholic community, became hotter and hotter under the collar over a cause that was not political but religious, a fact that gave much more force to their convictions.

The spectacular blunder in question was to blame the demonstrators at Corpus Christi for burning a flag. It was known straightaway that they had not been involved, that it had actually been burnt in a police station in the area. The incident tipped the scales for groups from the Air Force and Navy who subsequently decided to bring forward a coup d'état already in the pipeline.

The rest is common knowledge: the bombing of the Plaza de Mayo and consequent massacre of 200 to 300 people who happened to be passing through. The organisers were in fact trying to kill Perón, who was at the War Ministry. All hell was let loose on Buenos Aires and other cities in the provinces that night. Churches were burnt and looted and Perón was incapable of putting a stop to it. As a result, the noonday events in the Plaza de Mayo, a desperate homicidal bombardment that killed hundreds of people, was overshadowed by churches burning in the night. This happened at a time when nothing so much as moved in Argentina without the government's knowledge. If the arson had not been ordered directly by the ruling party, it did at least have its complicity along with that of the fire brigade and the police, in short the forces of repression.

From then on Perón's attitude in 1953 resurfaced. After some extremely rigorous measures against his opponents an amnesty followed. While Argentina was awaiting the government backlash against the men who had tried to kill its president and instead killed so many people in the Plaza de Mayo, Perón launched a peace offensive. Once again he offered his opponents the chance of coming into the political fold. He even offered, in his words, to resign the leadership of the Revolution and become President of the Nation and allowed his opponents to voice their opinions on radio for the first time. On 31 July 1955 the first voice to be heard was Frondizi's.

The great nineteenth century historian, de Tocqueville, said something very apt in this respect: the most difficult moment for bad governments is when they begin to reform. It was not that the Peronist regime had been bad across the board but a sense of omnipotence, harassment of opponents and a refusal to accept that they could be adversaries without being enemies were all strongly present. When Peronism rid itself of some of its more despised officials, when it gave opposition leaders the chance to be heard, then the system began to reel.

Perón's opponents received the offer of conciliation without much enthusiasm. They welcomed having a nationwide voice but did not in the slightest believe that the man was serious. Nevertheless, Perón changed his team. He parted with his Interior Minister, Angel

Borlenghi, with the czar of press and propaganda, Raúl Apold, with the chief of police... the mainstays of his regime. The summer of peacemaking lasted nearly two months until on August 31 all the radio stations reported that Perón was resigning as President of the Republic.

Before a crowd in the Plaza de Mayo he launched into an utter shambles of a speech, another of those inscrutable blunders. I have spoken to some of the participants. Oscar Albrieu, his interior minister, says that he spoke to Perón at midday: he was calm and composed but after lunch was quite the reverse, capable of threatening to do away with all his enemies in that famous "five against one" speech still so clear in Argentinians' memories; a speech which, after the purge of the Armed Forces, drove a small group of conspirators who thought there was no other way out to take to the streets. Either they prepared for a death sentence or they took to the streets to try and oust the regime.

On 16 September 1955 General Lonardi staged an extremely puzzling revolt in Córdoba. The retired Lonardi with no troops under his command was convinced that all he had to do was establish an anti-Peronist stronghold and hold it for two or three days, enough time for the military situation to erupt. If one stops to think, apart from the navy who were unanimously against Perón, opinion was equally divided in the rest of the armed forces: in the Army almost all units backed the government and there were also many units in the Air Force who supported Perón. Yet a revolt in Córdoba and its message of strength and hope broadcast to its sympathisers nationwide was enough for the regime to collapse of its own accord.

Furthermore, nobody went out onto the streets to defend Perón (who did nothing to encourage it either). He claimed he had wanted to arm the workers but a minister, General Humberto Sosa Molinas, had opposed him. According to other statements made later in exile, he did not want to fight for fear of causing irreparable damage.

Also remarkable were the decisiveness of these men who christened the rebellion the *Revolución Libertadora* or "Liberating Revolution", the puzzling halfheartedness of the forces supposedly supporting Perón and the way Perón himself behaved. He first set up headquarters at the War Ministry and tried to lead operations himself, then shut himself away in his presidential residence and eventually issued a highly ambiguous statement which was analysed by the generals until a younger group of officers urged them to consider the document as a resignation.

I will not get bogged down in the complexities of the situation, first and foremost because they are not pleasant and secondly because there is not much proof. What I am referring to is Perón's private behaviour towards the end of his second presidency. It was almost as if Evita's absence had deprived him of some inner resilience. He might have been hated by his opponents but he could not be disrespected: he had been a sober, hard-working man who clearly enjoyed his work and whose private life was beyond reproach. After Evita's death he began to keep company with a group of girls from the *UES* secondary school and his subsequent affair with a sweet little fourteen-year-old (he was nearly sixty at the time) was well-known. He installed her in the presidential residence and treated her like a sweetheart. He would even take her to events such as the cinema festival in Mar del Plata in April 1954 or boxing matches. Just as notorious as this relationship were his sorties on a motor scooter.

I believe that these attitudes cooled the masses' love for Perón. I do not mean that people stopped loving him but they did stop respecting him. This is why they did not come forward to defend his achievements and their own quality of life. Argentinian workers were conspicuously better off by the end of Perón's government. The purchasing power of their salary had distinctly improved and the social, touristic and welfare dimensions of the trades unions were making themselves felt. Pensions, which by late 1954 only benefited a handful of professions, had been extended. True, Perón had financed his Second Five-Year Plan by skimming money off the Pension Fund but it is also true that this situation could have lasted several years longer. People undoubtedly lived better under Perón and yet in these days when the government's collapse was imminent, the higher standard of living did not translate into gratitude for the man who made such things possible. The fact is that on September 20 the generals accepted the resignation and shortly afterwards Perón took refuge in the Paraguayan Embassy. This chapter of Peronism was closed.

One last comment: when Perón was forced to seek asylum in Paraguay he was probably the most discredited man in Argentina even among his own supporters who were accusing him, an acting general, of not defending his system. He had also overstepped the mark in his private relationships; unpleasant aspects of his government had come to light and yet 18 years later Perón returned. Which just goes to show that in politics you never can tell.

CHAPTER XIV THE LIBERATING REVOLUTION

The phrase Revolución Libertadora, *commonly used by historians and political scientists, tends to provoke in them different reactions according to how they view Perón and his regime. Quite apart from these feelings, we must here distinguish between the uprising of 1955 and the subsequent government, both of which made use of the phrase 'Liberating Revolution'.*

This will be my last strictly historical chapter for I intend to devote the final chapter to reviewing what we have seen. But I must warn the reader that this chapter is full of prickly issues with subjective implications. I shall try to be as honest as possibly, though demanding absolute objectivity of a historian, and a contemporary one at that, is unrealistic.

I shall try to examine these events without passion or bias and to excise any bias or passion I might once have had. I will say right out that I belonged to the half of Argentina who greeted the 1955 coup as a liberation, the end of a nightmare. Still, I have tried over the years to put my personal feelings behind me in order to have a comprehensive, unblinkered grasp of the other half.

SEPTEMBER 1955

One of the mysteries of our contemporary history is how Lonardi, with such scant means at his disposal, procured such a swift victory, and by correlation why Perón, apparently at the height of his powers, went under so quickly? I believe the answer must be sought in the realms of the spirit: Perón was defeated emotionally in September 1955, while Lonardi and his men were determined to triumph at all costs.

Lonardi had the whole of the Navy behind him but this was never a decisive factor. His actions were based on the idea that establishing a strategic focus for revolt would be enough to bring down the Peronist edifice. Perón, who in the weeks leading up to the coup had alternately been playing the peacemaker and warmonger, found that that the armed columns he sent to Córdoba were reluctant to go. The planes (the famous 'pancakes' as they were known) were turning back and Perón had misgivings about his generals. He did not arm the unions as he had so often promised to, instead remaining silent and hardly directing operations.

In his book *Dios es justo* (God is Just) Lonardi's son tells us that his father's slogan was "act with maximum brutality." The rebels felt they were laying their lives on the line and Perón's rash words of August 1 promised as much. However, officially, the secretary of the *CGT* called for calm.

To my mind this was all a consequence of Perón's long reign. He had inevitably made mistakes, isolated himself from broad swathes of society, and his cause had lost its vitality and faith. It is undoubtedly true that he still had half the country behind him but it is also true that nobody took to the streets to defend him and that statements issued by the ruling party did not inspire resistance.

The apparently unshakeable Peronist power structure collapsed in four days under the weight of nothing more than a handful of advancing warships (which at best could fire a few broadsides) and a Lonardi under siege in Córdoba. It is a political lesson about flagging energy in prolonged government and the need for any political enterprise to be animated by spiritual dynamism.

In the early morning of September 16 the retired General and a small group of young officers set up their headquarters in the vicinity of the city of Córdoba. At the same time part of the fleet set sail from Puerto Belgrano bound for the River Plate. By early morning on September 21, General Juan Perón was seeking shelter in the Paraguayan Embassy. The Liberating Revolution had triumphed almost without a struggle and the decade-long Peronist experiment was drawing to an end.

On a completely personal note, after years of consideration, I believe the Liberating Revolution was a bad thing for Argentina. If it had not taken place, Perón would have had to introduce reforms and broaden the scope of those begun in July. Thus his mandate would probably have ended with defeat at the ballot box, but being defeated by the coup meant instead that his adjustments did not have a chance to play themselves out. The use of force ushered in a long line of weak, limited constitutional governments and de facto regimes which invariably ended in failure. This is clear to us now but at the time it was a question of all or nothing and it did not occur to half the country, who like me rejoiced at Perón's fall from grace, that the overthrow of a constitutional government is never positive.

Before turning the page I wish to add two things about our political culture. One is the fact that Perón sought asylum and admitted defeat virtually without a fight. His enemies said he acted out of cowardice; he himself later explained that he had not wanted blood to be spilled or national assets to be destroyed. Whatever, Perón's attitude did save Argentinians much suffering, since the revolution could have resulted in a real civil war.

The second also has to do with Perón taking refuge on a Paraguayan gunboat. I know for a fact that there were plans afoot among the most fanatical "gorillas" (as Perón's opponents were known) to storm or sink the small boat. The de facto government authorities steadfastly opposed this insanity and the Foreign Secretary, Mario Amadeo, personally helped the ex-president in getting the right of asylum to be respected across the board. Even in the middle of such bitter animosity there was enough good sense or good luck to set certain limits and uphold respect for the rule of law.

LONARDI, OR THWARTED IDEALISM

On September 22 General Eduardo Lonardi swore himself in as provisional president. His cabinet was a faithful reflection of the forces that had accompanied him, though rather a mixed bag: from out-and-out liberals to nationalist Catholics who had clashed with Perón over his treatment of the Church. Lonardi was a retired soldier with no political experience nor much in the way of civilian relations, but he did have a plan which he presented clearly to those close to him, namely that his provisional administration was to be short; that there would be no "winners or losers" and that solutions that did no harm to Peronism had to be found.

It was an unworkable agenda. Many people who supported the new Liberating government nursed grudges, legitimate or otherwise, against the fallen regime and were clamouring for justice. Besides Peronism had been assembling the state and para-state apparatus for nearly ten years and it did not stand to reason that this would remain in place: those who had been discharged and imprisoned for the 1951 coup were demanding their reinstatement to the ranks; the old owners of *La Prensa* were demanding their property back; civil servants laid off for political reasons wanted to go back to work. Anti-Peronist hard-liners were pressing for a witch-hunt in the Peronist Party, the *CGT* and the main unions but Lonardi held out against them time and time again.

Lonardi would have needed all the personal qualities of Roca, Yrigoyen and Perón rolled into one to be able to realise his well-intentioned aims. But he was a man of simple goodwill who had no support to speak of either in anti-Peronist or revolutionary circles. Moreover, he made mistakes in choosing his close collaborators, some of whom were pro-Fascist.

At the beginning of November, under relentless pressure from his colleagues calling for strenuous measures to 'de-Peronise' the country, his War Minister was forced to resign. Lonardi was then forced to share power with the generals. He refused and was overthrown without offering any resistance in an unexpected but inevitable palace coup. Months later, removed from public life, Lonardi died. He was already seriously ill when he took office, though his unflagging will-power had allowed him to get through these difficult times without showing any signs of his deteriorating health.

ARAMBURU, OR AN END TO AMBIGUITIES

The new provisional president, General Pedro E. Aramburu, had led the plot to overthrow Perón. In early September he did not feel he could muster the necessary forces and turned down the leadership, which Lonardi immediately accepted. Aramburu played a rather lacklustre role in the Liberating Revolution finally taking up the post of army Chief of Staff. He then moved to the chief magistracy with the backing of the more revanchist military groups and liberal civilian forces.

With Aramburu any remaining ambiguities ceased. There were winners and there were losers. The Peronist Party, the *CGT* and most of the unions were invaded by government appointees. The use of symbols relating to the deposed regime was banned and many political and union leaders were arrested. Being a supporter of Perón after November 1955 was no joke.

In terms of the de facto regime's early policy, Aramburu simply stated that elections would come "not a minute too soon nor a minute too late" and this vague promise set the public's mind at rest regarding any ambitions he might have to remain in power.

Those around Aramburu thought the Argentinian political equation was relatively easy to solve: it was simply a question of showing the country the Justicialist regime's huge confidence trick. Given time people would stop being Peronist and elections could be called in the knowledge that future presidents would support the Liberating Revolution and uphold its values.

But people's support for their exiled leader did not lessen. They ignored the reports of shady deals, orgies and blunders preferring instead to remember Perón's achievements, the succour provided by the Eva Perón Foundation, their happiness at enjoying previously unaffordable benefits such as holidays, union health and benefits schemes and a better standard of living.

A few Peronist activists attempted to set up a resistance network with only limited success. In the newly supervised trades unions a new generation of leaders replaced the opportunists who had enjoyed the perks of power at Perón's side but had not defended him when the time came. The ex-president himself sent demented instructions from Caracas and later Santo Domingo about armed resistance, sabotage and terrorism against the de facto government. None of this prompted the simple people to express their rejection of the Liberating Revolution en masse but their loyalty to Perón remained as steadfast as ever.

There were moments when Aramburu's 'gorilla' advisers had cause to think 'de-Peronisation' would be successful. The decision to eradicate Peronist feeling wherever possible was expressed on two occasions during 1956. The first was in May when the provisional government repealed the 1949 Constitution, reinstated the Constitution of 1853 and promised to call a constitutional convention in due time to update it.

The other occasion is associated with one of the most tragic instants in Argentina's recent history. In June 1956 a group of retired soldiers with Peronist affiliations attempted a coup at various points of the country. The uprising was put down and the provisional government imposed martial law and decreed execution by firing squad for anyone carrying a gun. Though the resistance had been quashed, more than thirty Argentinians, soldiers and civilians, and the uprising's leader, General Juan J. Valle, were shot.

It was over a hundred years since anyone had been executed for political reasons. Although there were those who applauded the measure, in general the severity of the punishment provoked wide, tacit condemnation. Nevertheless, the bloodbath was clear evidence that the leaders of the Liberating Revolution were irrevocably committed to their ultimate objectives.

THE BIG ISSUES

In the meantime, significant developments were going on at the heart of society. One of the most significant of these was an eruption of freedom of speech. Like any authoritarian regime Peronism did not make it easy to bring up the country's problems. Officially everything was going swimmingly and if anything went wrong Perón would fix it, an illusion that was kept up throughout Peron's terms in office by controlling the mass media.

The Liberating Revolution, however, opened up free discussion when it handed the official newspapers and magazines over to various political and ideological groups, excluding Peronism of course. The big issues facing Argentina very soon came to the fore: the State's future role in the economy, the oil supply, the role of foreign capital, education, industrial and agricultural policy, Argentina's place on the world stage and so on and so forth.

The provisional government 's policies were never very clearly defined in most of these areas. This was inevitable first and foremost because of internal differences but also because of precarious external circumstances. It had endorsed the Prebisch Report but had not carried out its recommendations. It dissolved some of the previous system's highly dubious organisations (the *IAPI* for example) but it hardly touched Perón's state apparatus. It adhered to the IMF but its foreign policy was extremely contradictory. It set up a duty-free zone in Patagonia, harshly criticised at the time. It looked sympathetically on the Yadarola Plan for turning *YPF* into a contractor of foreign oil companies but did not take the matter any further.

The frank discussions on the major issues surrounding Argentina's future were one of the most positive aspects of Aramburu's presidency and kept pace with a shift of attitude being experienced in almost all major parties. For, now that Peronism had apparently been persecuted out of existence, dissent in the remaining parties reigned supreme, in some cases leading to outright division.

This was only logical. During the decade of Peronism, the opposition parties had had to survive by maintaining unity at all costs. Anything else would have been suicidal. With Perón gone, internal conflicts, differing viewpoints and even personal ambitions burst onto the scene as virulently as the eagerness to debate and discuss had been repressed under his regime.

Socialism split into two camps, Conservatism into three and at the beginning of 1957 the *UCR*, the main opposition, which had maintained a strained but ostensible unity, became two separate parties, a pro-government one led by Ricardo Balbín and an anti-government one led by Arturo Frondizi, which looked more like Peronism with its advanced sloganeering to seduce young people, intellectuals and progressive groups.

BLOOD COUNTS AND PRESIDENTIAL ELECTIONS

In early 1957 Aramburu's government called constituent delegate elections. Announced for July, these elections served two purposes, one institutional and the other political. For one thing it was imperative to endorse the overturning of the 1949 Constitution, which had been performed by simple decree. Besides that, it would be a tentative opinion poll (or "blood count" as it was referred to at the time) for any future general elections.

The ballot was disappointing for the leaders of the Revolution. From Caracas Perón had ordered his faithful to spoil their votes by returning blank ballot papers, and protest voting subsequently accounted for 24 percent of all votes cast. Peronism continued in the majority, Balbín's *UCR del Pueblo* (People's Radical Civic Union) was next with a similar percentage and Frondizi's *UCR Intransigente* (Intransigent Radical Civic Union) took 21 percent. Since Argentina had proportional representation, the Constituent Convention should have reflected the pluralism of the party scene (though it goes without saying that Peronism remained on the sidelines, despite the presence of maverick delegates previously from the Peronist ranks).

The Convention met in Santa Fe and representatives siding with Frondizi impugned its validity. Their subsequent withdrawal left the meeting with a strict quorum, a welcome decision for the Peronists who, by their spoiling votes, had also impugned the meeting. Nevertheless, the assembly did manage to ratify the 1853 Constitution with an addendum to Article 14 containing new social practices. The Convention then broke up. This was a prelude to the crucial election campaign, a campaign that would decide Argentina's fate for several years to come. 23 February 1958 was the date set by Aramburu for general elections for president, vice-president, governors, senators, deputies and so on.

Seldom has there been such intense political activity in Argentina. Frondizi was constantly canvassing the Peronists to gain the electoral support he so desperately needed while at the same time working up an agenda that would satisfy the most disparate interests such as laymen and Catholics, industrialists and liberals, advocates of a pro-

Western approach and leftist sympathisers. He was a unique political figure with his unheard-of promises of a development plan "for twenty million Argentinians".

Balbín on the other hand had to tread an extremely narrow path between his support for the de facto government and his election needs. There were half a dozen other candidates but opinion was divided between the two Radical leaders, who seven years earlier had stood together against Perón in his bid for re-election. They had now become fierce opponents.

Meanwhile Perón was in a quandary. He could not be sure that his faithful following would once again spoil their votes since it was now a question of electing constitutional authorities to govern the country for seven years with thousands of posts at stake at all levels of government. Not taking part could have meant a massive waning of his influence. It was also becoming clear that the average Peronist was leaning towards Frondizi with his harsh criticisms of Aramburu's administration and his promises to respect the workers' movement and bring this phase of hatred and revenge to an end.

Did a pact really exist between Perón and Frondizi? Although Frondizi always emphatically denied ever having signed any electoral agreement, conversations between the *UCRI* candidate's close associates and the exiled Perón in Santo Domingo did undeniably take place. Also undeniable is the fact that two weeks before the country went to the polls Perón ordered his followers to vote for Frondizi. At all events the historical puzzle is irrelevant since Frondizi would have won anyway, though probably with less of a landslide.

Thus on 23 February 1958, 49 percent of voters ordained Frondizi as president. His nearest rival got 29 percent and spoiled votes counted for a mere 8 percent. Frondizi's party won all the governorships, the entire Senate and two thirds of the Congress. Never had such a momentous victory been seen in Argentina. In the future, however, support for the outlawed Peronist Party would prove to be a thorn in his side.

Of course, this was not in evidence in the eventful days after the election amidst all the winning party's euphoria and the general public's feeling that the country had finally taken the road towards permanent normalisation. Despite reports of the Revolutionary government's intention to refuse to recognise the elections, Aramburu rushed to greet Frondizi as president elect and to reiterate his willingness to hand over power.

On 1 May 1958 Arturo Frondizi did indeed receive the sash and sceptre of power and prepared to shoulder his new responsibilities. And here I must bring our story to a close.

INHERITED BURDENS

One or two closing remarks to reflect on. Apart from its organisers' intentions, the Liberating Revolution and the ensuing provisional government had extremely negative repercussions. At the beginning of the chapter, I mentioned that the outbreak of the revolution in September 1955 saved Perón from having to make any significant adjustments to the more symbolic aspects of his policies. So which is the real Perón? The man who nationalised the railways or the man who was negotiating a massive oil concession in Patagonia? The man advocating a third position or the man desperately seeking the United States' backing? The man seeking social justice or the man cutting back on social achievements in the Productivity Congress? The peacemaker or the aggressor? The Revolution saved Perón from falling into ever steeper decline and from failing to act according to his beliefs but the insurgents themselves had no truck with such considerations. For them overthrowing Perón was a question of life or death that could not be put off.

However, the blackest consequence of the Liberating Revolution lies in the attitude of the Armed Forces inasmuch as they took on the role of strict custodians of anti-Peronism. This was the main reason for the countless demands Frondizi had to put up with during his presidency and for his eventual overthrow in 1962. Their anti-Peronism led the military to win over José María Guido so that the elections presided over by this modest patriot guaranteed a completely Peronism-free government. The threat of yet another Peronist victory also helped in Arturo Illia's overthrow of 1966, since the aim of Juan Carlos Onganía's de facto regime was to freeze politics until "the curse" of Peronism began to subside.

The Armed Forces were determined not to let the slightest hint of Peronism resurface anywhere and this determination distorted the democratic process by bringing with it a series of weak constitutional governments tainted by illegitimacy and military regimes that invariably ended in failure.

Banned and lacking the means for political expression, Peronism sought alternatives in order to continue on the national stage. It found them in the trades union movement: this was how the *CGT* or the *62 Organizaciones* became an unofficial Peronist Party. The union movement prodded, pushed and pressurised the way any opposition would but without the usual institutional controls that restrain political parties, which also seriously distorted and weakened the governments of Frondizi and Illia and was a source of conflict for Onganía. In other words, after the Liberating Revolution politics were unrecognisable: the Armed Forces became an anti-Peronist police force and the workers' movement turned into a militant Peronist Party.

This outline is perhaps on the simplistic side but I believe that it is broadly accurate. So-called Anti-Peronist "gorillaism" cast a shadow over Argentinian life. It led to a distrust of democracy in the interests of a mythical national revolution, a socialist homeland and other pernicious utopias. This is not to disown the part Perón played in encouraging gorillaism in reverse. The truth of the matter is that after the Liberating Revolution the country was ungovernable because of Peronism.

When examining these years, one realises that hatred and the desire for revenge were the prevalent feelings. With its high-handed authoritarianism when in office, Peronism had sown abundant seeds and the liberators gave back more than they got in terms of resentment. These forces were not adversaries but true enemies. Each refused to recognise anything positive in the other. The blighted harvest reaped by Argentinian society was long and bitter. Only time would find a remedy for our gruelling affliction; time that is, and the robust spirit of most Argentinians that usually predominates when we are not artificially driven to violence or intolerance.

CHAPTER XV HISTORY LESSONS

Right at the beginning I said that trying to summarise Argentinian history in fifteen chapters is almost sacrilege because historical processes are always intricately interrelated. Any attempt to simplify them in a way betrays the goals of accuracy and faithfulness that must inspire the historian. But it is also true that history is by definition boundless, ungraspable, untellable. Therefore, my intention to outline some of the more fundamental aspects of Argentinian history (many others have stayed in the inkwell) is also valid.

I have tried to convey the processes that have at every step founded the Argentina we live in today, beginning with the most distant events and closing at a point where our own lives merge into any retelling. Here it has seemed wise to put the last full-stop.

In this last chapter it would seem appropriate to talk about what might be called "history lessons". I am fully aware that history does not instruct, is not life's mistress. If history were truly the mistress of life, as in the oft-repeated words from Cicero's De Oratore *(which we all know to be a little white lie, a courtesy to historians), then the mistakes by societies' leaders would not be committed and we historians would not only be the advisers but the unerring high priests of the governors and the governed... I have entitled this chapter "History Lessons" but its modest contents are simply a kind of historian's balance-sheet.*

FEDERALISM

I mentioned that historical processes are composed of both ruptures and continuities. The interplay of the two forces is in a manner of speaking the counterpoint that draws together the great symphony of Argentinian history (and I might add, universal history).

One of the most striking continuities is the Argentinian people's will to organise themselves federally, not only in political but in social terms too: the life of the community as a whole is affected by our distinctive regional, provincial and local identities.

We have seen this repeatedly throughout our account. Ever since Buenos Aires was founded these two Argentinas have been at odds in one way or another. If there is a dialectic in our history it lies in the confrontations and rapprochements between the region of influence around the River Plate and the land-locked North, Northwest, Cuyo and, later on, Patagonia.

Argentina is a federal country by both constitution and vocation yet its geographical arrangement condemns it to centralism and to dependence on Buenos Aires. So how can a nation with a single gateway to the outside world develop into a collection of autonomous entities? In Judge Matienzo's mind this gateway to the land became a kind of toll office and its occupants, the people or the *Porteño* ruling classes, charged dearly for keeping the door open, ajar or locked...

Rosas was not far wrong when in his letter from the Hacienda de Figueroa he said that Argentina and the United States were quite different cases. The latter's federal system evolved quite naturally from the seaports of the thirteen founding colonies whereas here the only seaport is Buenos Aires. Given this geographical drawback, history has shown the Argentinian people's genius for federalism, a genius that has been enshrined in our Constitution.

Nevertheless, when all is said and done, Argentina is a centralised country and Buenos Aires rules the roost. "This is Castille, that maketh and unmaketh men," said the old Spanish ballad book and Buenos Aires makes and unmakes economic and political policy, governments and prestige. The *Revolución del Parque* or the 1930 and 1943 revolutions were exclusively *Porteño* uprisings yet their effects were felt nationwide.

Will this trend ever be reversed? History lessons show us that true federalism is increasingly becoming a pipe dream. But they also show us that men of daring and imagination can find alternatives to suffocating centralism. I have been an ardent supporter of moving the Federal Capital from Buenos Aires and said as much in early 1982 in my book *Buenos Aires y el país* (Buenos Aires and Argentina). Raúl Alfonsín did not present the case for transferring the capital to Viedma properly. Argentinian society and even his own party received his proposals with little enthusiasm, a significant factor in his downfall. But I do still feel that moving the three government functions to another city, either existing now or to be built, is something that will become increasingly imperative. It will not entirely solve the problem of centralism but it will be an important palliative measure.

For now we must bear in mind that our vocation for federalism is an authentic one whose historical roots run deep. I believe that if there is a lesson to be learnt from a knowledge of our history it is the crucial federalist principle, the right of our regions to grow unconstrained and not have their assets and human resources swallowed up by our beloved, seductive monster, Buenos Aires.

DEMOCRACY

I would like to mention another constant flowing through our history, namely, the trend towards more democracy, a phenomenon that goes hand in hand with a trend towards truer egalitarianism. This trend can be distinguished at various times in the colonial period but after 1810 it is impossible to miss.

I said at the time that the May uprising brought about major changes in people's thinking, one of which was the replacement of the scholastic idea of the common good by the sovereignty of the people but it was a long time before this principle bore any practical fruit. At one time democracy consisted of nothing more than the *caudillo*'s capacity to lead his people, or "for every spear, a vote..." as the saying went.

As the country gradually evolved legal and political formulas were found so that the people's talent for democracy would be channelled peacefully. This was to culminate in the Sáenz Peña Law, which however did not automatically bring with it perfect democracy. The Law was often ignored and the legitimate and peaceful expression of the people's will at the polls was sometimes steam-rollered by military experiments, as we have seen.

Nevertheless, the Argentinian people are clearly cut out for democracy. Historically, the type of person emerging from the colonial period was a free agent who reacted badly to hierarchy or authority. Buenos Aires was a plebeian city with no aristocracy and in the provinces the predominant caste-like society was soon modified, especially after the mid-nineteenth century. The big immigrations later accentuated this levelling: the immigrants who came over to fulfil their aims in life to the best of their abilities relied solely on their own stamina and good luck; their children were educated under the system set up in the 1880s and soon took their place under the Argentinian sun.

Our history then shows an undeniable trend towards democracy. True it is that more recently there might have been assent shown towards authoritarian solutions or ones not in accord with plebiscites but these interregna have always been viewed as temporary if painful cures (though in some people's minds necessary ones). And afterwards, when elections were called, the Argentinian electorate has always delightedly voted en masse. Historically we are inseparable from democracy.

The same is true of our sense of egalitarianism, which also has a long history. Nineteenth-century travellers admired the straightforwardness with which labourers treated their employers, a very different attitude from the servility they saw elsewhere in the Americas. An Italian immigrant who settled in Colonia Caroya to the north of Córdoba in around 1870 wrote to relatives in his *paese* about the fact that it was not necessary to doff your hat when talking to rich men.

Egalitarianism does not mean that we all think of ourselves as being equal but that everyone should have equal opportunities to fulfil their potential, that nobody falls behind for lack of an education, that nobody is spurned for want of wealth, that a minimum of dignity is everybody's birthright. This is perhaps why Perón's idea of social justice was after an initial period of confrontation accepted by everyone. And why the laws enshrining the principle that the State cannot be indifferent to the fate of those less fortunate continued in force after his overthrow.

The related principles of democracy and egalitarianism run right through our history. They may at times have stumbled or been interrupted but they have never been cancelled. To do so would be to act against the nature of our society. Not all countries in Latin America can say the same.

CONFLICT AND HARMONY

Also discernible in our history is a dual process of harsh confrontation and intelligent, tolerant agreement. In a book I wrote several years ago I referred to this duality as *Conflict and Harmony*, a title I borrowed from one of Sarmiento's later works.

Happily enough the kind of harrowing struggles that have bathed so many of our Latin American brothers in blood have not taken place in Argentina, or have done so very circumstantially. Nevertheless, our political battles have on occasion been intense: Unitarians versus Federals, Radicals versus Conservatives, Peronists versus gorillas.

There have been times when Argentinians have felt divided and when these divisions were real. Meaningful values will suddenly appear and deep conflicts arise around them. I do not mean to invalidate these conflicts or the people who get mixed up in them. A follower of Yrigoyen at the turn of the century was ready to give his life in the revolution his leader was organising because he was fighting for the people's sovereignty and his right to vote. It is to be respected, and a man of the stature of Pellegrini said as much when the amnesty for the 1905 revolutionaries was under discussion.

Such confrontations serve to clarify matters and define values. Ideally they should result in compliance with the only arbitration a democracy should respect, namely, the will of the people peacefully and freely expressed at the ballot box. Then come the pacts, agreements, conciliation schemes and alliances. One side gives a little ground in order to clear up situations that might otherwise get out of hand.

The 1853 Constitution was just such an agreement: a formula for compromise between provinces at loggerheads. The Sáenz Peña Law was also a kind of pact, whose subtext was a signal from the Regime to the Radicals along the lines of "Give up your revolution, come out of abstention and vote and we will guarantee you free suffrage, endorse your victory if you win and govern with you if you lose."

This oscillation from conflict to harmony punctuates the whole of our history. One has to admire both men like Alem or de la Torre, who played leading roles in confrontation and those who, like Roca or Ortiz, implemented agreement and conciliation, for our political history is cut from both kinds of cloth. Life lived only in confrontation is impossible: every society at some stage demands peace and fellowship. "A nation's existence is ... a regular daily plebiscite," said Renan and such a plebiscite can only make its presence felt if the validity of other people's opinions is acknowledged, however remote from or contrary to one's own.

Still, neither can life be based on constant understanding, a lesson to be learnt from the *Roquistas*, who demeaned themselves with constant power-sharing and immoral pacts. There are moments for civilised confrontation and there are moments for honourable agreement, too. But it should be remembered that the best agreement is respect for the Constitution and the law. This is what establishes the sacred, inviolable rules of the game.

One must not fear conflict; instead, one should try not to let it get out of hand. But neither must one turn one's back on the harmony constituted by codes and customs, languages and gestures, myth and reality and so on. A nation's wisdom probably consists in knowing how to mete out its conflicts and agreements so that they bear lasting fruit.

This may all seem too theoretical and rhetorical. Nevertheless, throughout these pages I have been referring both to clashes and accords. Argentina has long experience in this area and history has much to teach us in the respect.

AMERICANS OR EUROPEANS?

Lastly, let us look at one of the most abiding features of Argentina. I am referring to our talent for affiliating ourselves with Europe, a vocation which has lasted from the days of Spanish domination until now.

You probably remember what I said early on about the River Plate's struggle to make its territory an absurdly expensive avenue for commodities being transported to Potosí. The struggle to get the ships supplying Alto Perú, Tucumán and Buenos Aires to import their merchandise via the South Atlantic and the River Plate lasted two centuries but meant stronger ties with Spain and therefore with Europe. The trend became more pronounced after the creation of the Vice-Royalty and the *Auto de Libre Comercio*, and intensified still further after 1810. It had occasional ups and downs until it became official government policy after Caseros.

So far I have not mentioned the Elizalde Memorandum. This was a document issued by Rufino de Elizalde, Mitre's Foreign Secretary, in reply to an invitation from his Peruvian counterpart to take part in a conference in Lima to put an end to hostilities being waged by certain powers against various Latin American nations in around 1864 or 1865. In his brutally frank reply Elizalde stated that Argentina had little to do with the rest of the Americas but expected a great deal from its relationship with Europe. He added that Argentina had only occasional problems with Old World nations, that they sent immigrants and capital and that he expected their contributions to grow more plentiful.

The Elizalde Memorandum admittedly established an intelligent policy that lasted through different governments and international climates for almost a century. Cuyo, the North and Northwest kept up the age-old commercial ties with their neighbours. But as Argentina gradually began to export products from the Pampas these ties weakened and almost disappeared. In short, Argentina was betting on its links with Europe.

This was an intelligent gamble and the only one capable of giving us immediate returns. Great Britain, France, Belgium and

Germany were good markets for our products but these and other countries on the old continent were also sending us people, capital, new technologies, goods and ideas that enriched us every step of the way. What could Latin America offer us? What exchange could possibly exist with countries, many of whom were unstable and conflict-ridden?

Things changed slowly after the Second World War. Britain lost its position as our partner and principal client. Europe began to close in on itself and set up barriers to our products, and we had to look for other markets. Yet Argentina still has a more European than Latin American feel about it because of these long-standing economic, commercial and financial ties and its ethnic make-up. The Mexican novelist Carlos Fuentes says that Mexicans came from the Aztecs, Peruvians from the Incas and Argentinians from the ships. Indeed, almost all of us can recall a grandfather or great-grandfather who arrived on a ship.

Let's be quite honest: we are hardly Latin American at all. Latin America only starts to appear north of Córdoba, where the chapels, faces or songs take us back to our pre-Hispanic origins. Argentinians have only lived one authentic Latin American moment, when San Martín crossed the Andes to free the Chileans and Peruvians. The rest is hot air, except perhaps for the deranged episode of the Malvinas War in 1982, when the only voices of encouragement came from other Latin American countries. Europe, who we were emotionally closer to, effectively turned its back on us. (They had every right to, mind you.) Still, I get the impression that, like me, many of my fellow Argentinians at the time realised that the only solidarity was coming from this continent, towards which we have been indifferent for so long...

So where do we go from here? I am not an expert or politician and am not obliged to say what Argentina's future on the world stage will be like. I do not know if we should turn our gaze away from Europe to integration with our neighbours as Mercosur is proposing, but I would like to underline that a constant in our history has been our inclination towards Europe. Perhaps the time has come to stress this propinquity or perhaps it is a question of opening other paths.

This strange multipolar world probably demands efforts other than imagination, efforts that I cannot and do not have to make.

I could go on with the list of constants offered up by study of our history but I shall just mention one more which has always drawn my attention, namely, Argentina's indebtedness.

Just fourteen years after the 1810 uprising as part of the United Provinces of the River Plate, our country had already acquired its first foreign accommodation from the famous Baring Brothers; it has gone down in history as the archetype of a useless, costly loan. Since then, with the exception of the Rosas years, Argentina has continually incurred financial commitments abroad. Urquiza incurred debts to save his Paraná government from financial ruin; Sarmiento was a past master at running up debts, and so were Roca and his followers. Perón, who in 1946 had repatriated the foreign debt, had to ask the United States for a special loan four years later. I shan't go on other than to mention the colossal increase in the foreign debt between 1976 and 1983 during the military dictatorship known as the *Proceso*.

Argentina has almost constantly been in debt. It has almost become a way of life. But there are good debts and bad debts and we have incurred both: bad debts like the ones taken out so that people can go to Miami or build themselves flats in Punta Del Este; good debts like the ones contracted towards the end of last century to buy wire fences, windpumps, seeds and so on in order to rationalise farming and agriculture. But the fact is that "the great debtor of the South" as Sarmiento called Argentina in a parody of the national anthem (conveniently ignoring his own part in amassing Argentina's debt) casts her shadow over our history.

In closing I would like to say a word about Argentina's geographical location. If we look at the globe, we can see how peripheral we are. We are situated at a vast distance from other continents and even in Latin America, here we sit dangling all this way down south.

Our location on this earth has its advantages and disadvantages. For a start, in the days of Spanish jurisdiction our remoteness entailed a certain lack of concern on the mother country's part, until the advent of the Bourbons, that is. Even nowadays we do not realise how peripheral our position is: the problems of the major world powers hardly affect us, for we are a long way from the eye of any political storms; this perception of ourselves, among other factors, must have played a part in contriving our neutral stance in the last two world wars. We can feel this distance when we check the figures for European tourists and realise how few come over. Or the high number of non-neighbouring countries we import from or export to.

Yet at the same time, Argentina's 4,000 kilometre north-south stretch contains every conceivable type of climate and produce. A hundred years ago Argentinians realised that the key to national success lay in taking advantage of the wealth the earth had provided them with. Today this diversity should occupy our imagination and best efforts in order to find new ways forward, new kinds of production, aided by an education which, despite deterioration, continues to give our people conspicuous qualities of mental agility and a flair for adapting to new situations.

GETTING TO KNOW OURSELVES

And so we are coming to the end of our voyage, which set out from Argentina's remote humble beginnings and has brought us to modern times. Looking back, the seas we have sailed have at times been stormy, at others calm.

I have attempted to be truthful and to set out the facts and their interpretations with integrity. It is worth restating the fact that, in matters historical, objectivity does not exist, since historians are only human beings from a given place with a given education and values. But there is a window of opportunity for honesty in a chronicle such as this and I can assure you I have been honest. I can also assure you I have had a great deal of fun.

What these pages leave you with I do not know. As a narrator of history they have been very useful to me because they have made me review and summarise processes that I have had to simplify for them to be comprehensible to a public that has not the slightest reason to be well-versed in them. To you the readers this fleeting glimpse of

Argentinian history may also have been of use, for getting to know the country you were born in or live in almost always means growing a little fonder of it, a little more understanding of its shortcomings, yet at the same time prouder of its better qualities.

Studying how this country, my country, was made always restores my inborn optimism. I can appreciate how huge difficulties and divisions were overcome, though the problems might have seemed insurmountable at the time. A solution was always found in the end. One way or another we always stayed afloat. I do not believe much in any one government but I do believe a great deal in my country, its sense of justice, its capacity for tolerance, its noble egalitarianism, its instinct for democracy and its intelligence.

This does not mean that I am being naïve but I am by no means a pessimist. Ours is a fine country and I hope these pages make it clear. At the end of the twentieth century the only thing Argentinians are short of is to deserve Argentina.

INDEX

CHAPTER VII

CHAPTER VIII

CHAPTER IX

CHAPTER X

CHAPTER XI

CHAPTER XII